AF577005

Gustav
Klimt

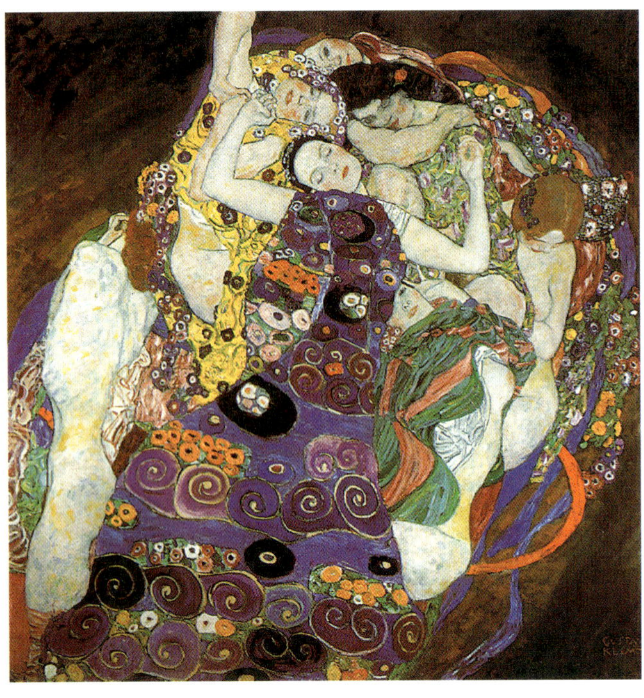

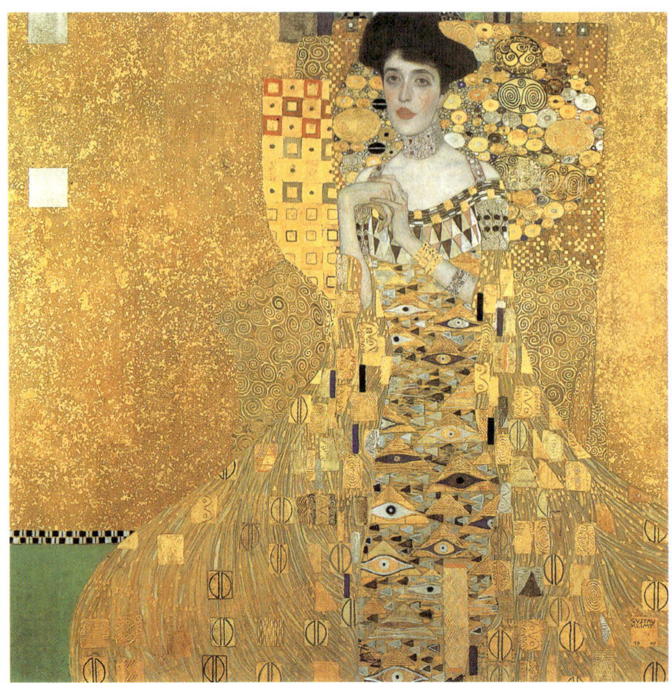

Published in 2004 by Grange Books
an imprint of Grange Books Plc
The Grange Kingsnorth Industrial Estate
Hoo, nr Rochester Kent ME3 9ND
www.Grangebooks.co.uk
ISBN 1-84013-652 9

Printed in China

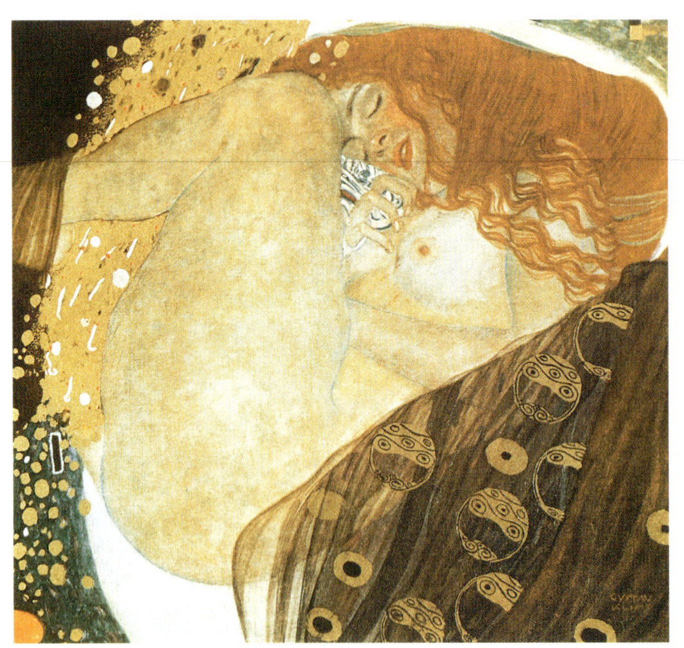

Gustav Klimt

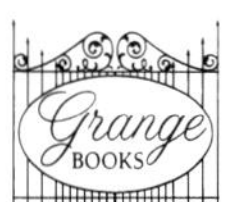

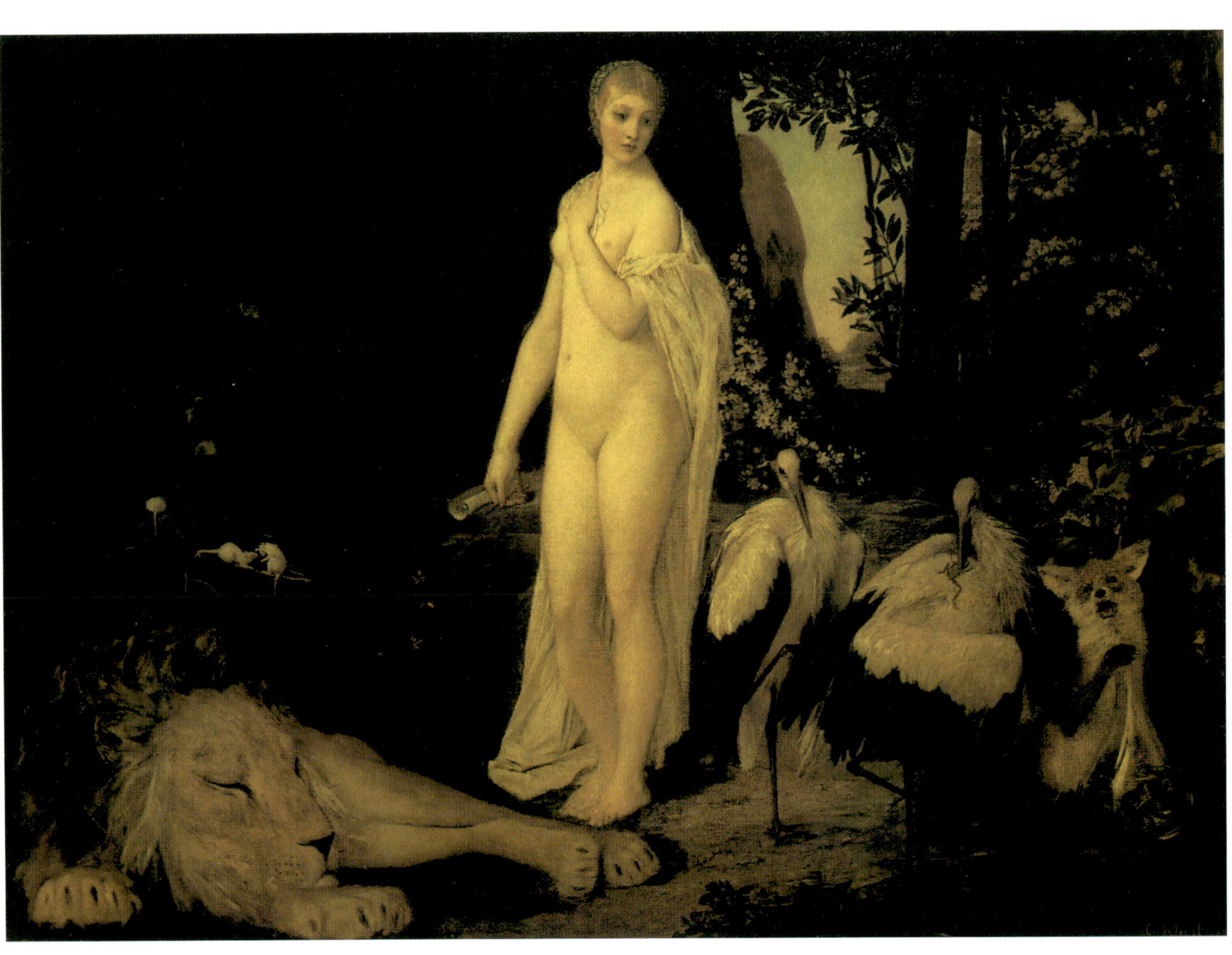

'I am not interested in myself as a subject for painting, but in others, particularly women...'

Beautiful, senuous and above all erotic, Gustav Klimt's paintings speak of a world of opulence and leisure, which seems aeons away from the harsh, post-modern environment we live in now. The subjects he treats - allegories, portraits, landscapes and erotic figures - contain virtually no reference to external events, but strive rather to create a world where beauty, above everything else, is dominant.

His use of colour and pattern, profoundly influenced by the art of Japan, ancient Egypt, and Byzantine Ravenna, the flat, two-dimensional perspective of his paintings, and the frequently stylized quality of his images form an oeuvre imbued with a profound sensuality and one where the figure of woman, above all, reigns supreme.

Beginnings

Klimt's very first works brought him success at an unusually early age. He came from a poor family where his father, a goldsmith and engraver, could scarcely maintain his wife and family of seven children.

Gustav, born in 1862, obtained a state grant to study at the Kunstgewerbeschule (the Vienna School of Arts and Crafts) at the age of 14. His talents as a draughtsman and painter were quickly noticed, and in 1879 he formed the Künstlercompagnie (Artists' Company) with his brother Ernst and another student, Franz Matsch.

The latter part of the nineteenth century was a period of great architectural activity in Vienna. In 1857, the Emperor Franz Joseph had ordered the destruction of the fortifications that had surrounded the medieval city centre.

The Ringstrasse was the result, a budding new district with magnificent buildings and beautiful parks, all paid for by public expenses.

Therefore, the young Klimt and his partners had ample opportunities to show their talents and they received early commissions to contribute to the decorations for the pageant organized to celebrate the silver wedding of the Emperor Franz Joseph and the Empress Elisabeth.

1. ***Fable***, 1883. Oil on canvas, 85 x 117 cm, Vienna, Historisches Museum.

In the following year, they were commissioned to produce a ceiling painting for the Thermal Baths in Carlsbad. Other public commissions soon followed.

When one examines these early works, such as *Fable* (p. 4), *The Idyll* (p. 7), or indeed one of Klimt's earliest drawings, *Male Nude* (p. 8), it is clear that he is a painter of great skill and promise, but remains entirely within the accepted contemporary norms in his depiction of academic and allegorical subjects.

The women in *Fable* and *Idyll* are plump, adroitly draped in plain textiles, their hair smoothly pulled back behind the neck.

Neither would look out of place in the eighteenth or even seventeenth century. Their sensuality is matronly, motherly, their nudity decorous rather than exciting.

In the past, pubic hair had - if this part of the body was revealed at all - traditionally been glossed over into a smooth and unsuggestive 'v' reminiscent of modern-day children's dolls.

Many early medieval or Renaissance paintings which had shown even the suggestion of male or female genitalia had suffered the absurd addition of a floating fig leaf painted in by later, more prudish, souls.

But even as early as 1896, Klimt had begun to be more explicit in the way he chose to depict the human figure.

There is, for example, an interesting difference between the final drawing for *Sculpture* and the painting itself. In the drawing we already see the trademark loose, wild, dark hair and the faintest traces of pubic hair.

The woman gazes directly at the viewer, standing as if caught naked in her bedroom doorway, summoning the viewer to caress her.

2. ***The Idyll***, 1884. Oil on canvas, 50 x 74 cm, Vienna, Historisches Museum.

The painting, by contrast, has reverted to a more traditional style: gone the frontal stance, back the classical sculptural pose. Up goes the hair and the pubic hair disappears.

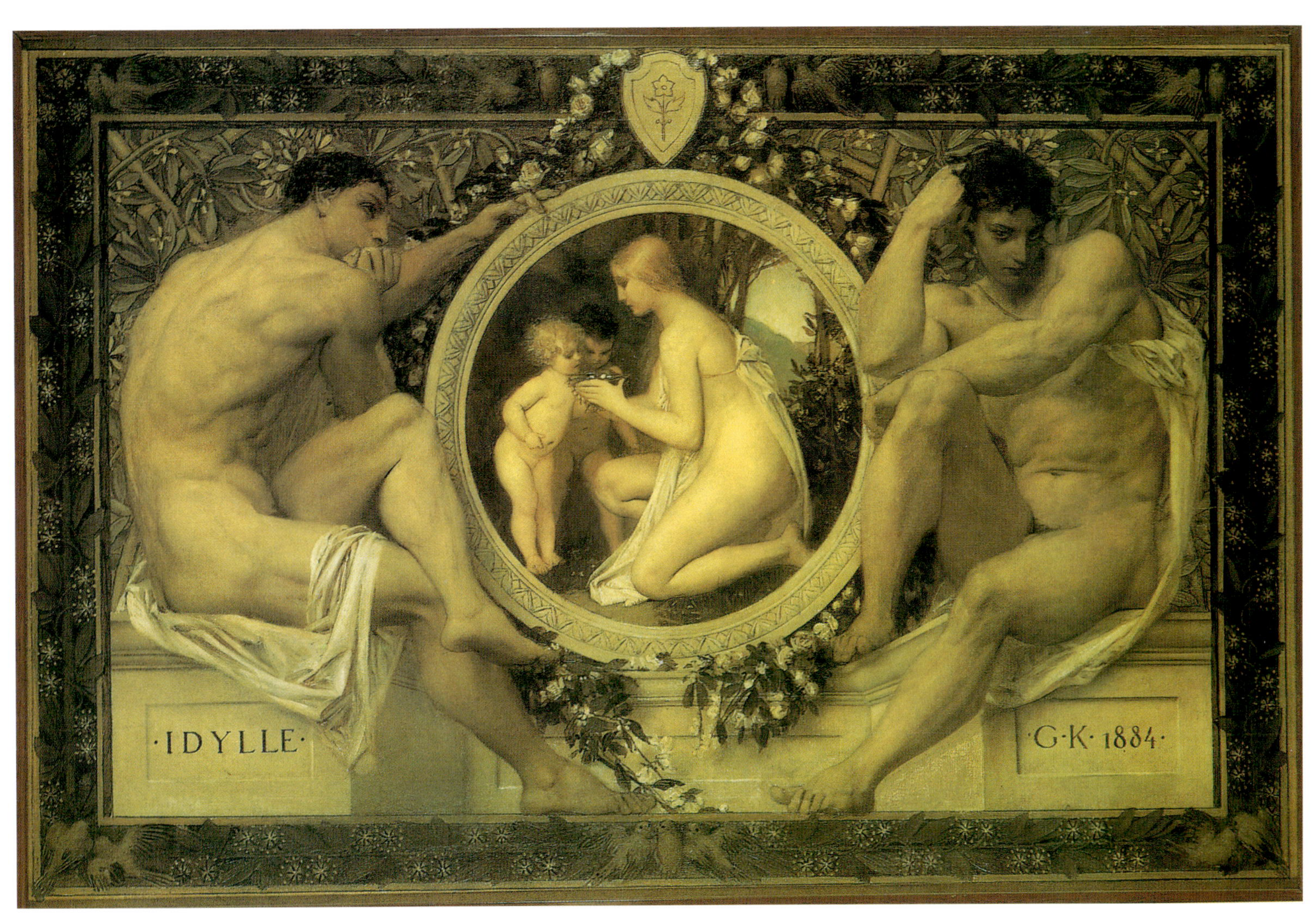
·IDYLLE·
·G·K·1884·

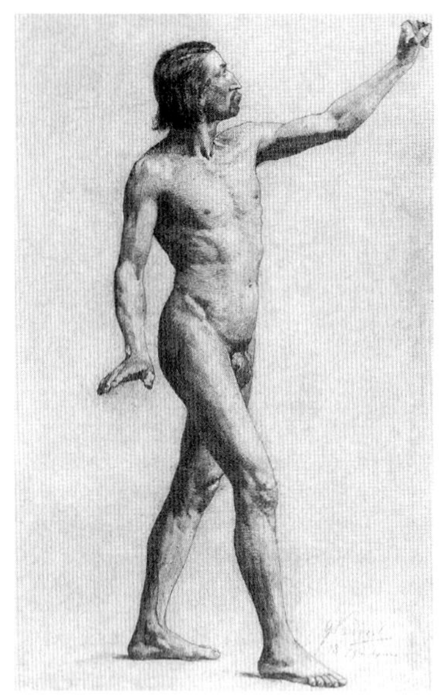

Secession

These early commissions established Klimt as a successful and prominent artist. Following the death of his father and brother Ernst in 1892, there seems to have been a distinct cooling-off in the working relationship between Klimt and Matsch as Klimt began to explore more adventurous waters.

In 1894, Matsch moved out of their communal studio, and in 1897 Klimt, together with his closest friends, resigned from the Künstlerhausgenossenschaft (the Co-operative Society of Austrian Artists) to form a new movement known as the Secession, of which he was immediately elected president.

The Secession was a great success, holding both a first and a second exhibition in 1898. The movement made enough money to commission their very own building, designed for them by the architect Joseph Maria Olbrich.

Above the entrance was their motto: 'To each age its art, to art its freedom'. The Secession not only came to represent the best of Austrian art, but was able to bring to Vienna French Impressionist and Belgian Naturalist works, which had never before been seen by the Austrian public.

Klimt was undoubtedly the central figure in this young and dynamic movement, but his success as a modern artist went hand in hand with the loss of his status as an acceptable establishment painter.

As he moved away from his traditional beginnings, he soon found himself at the centre of a series of scandals, which were to change his entire career.

Scandal

In 1894, Klimt and Matsch had received a commission to produce a series of paintings for the University of Vienna. The subjects Klimt was assigned were Philosophy, Medicine, and Jurisprudence.

The nature of the commission can be easily imagined: the university would be expecting a series of dignified, formal paintings in classical style depicting the wisdom of philosophers, the healing virtues of medicine, and doubtless a statuesque blindfolded female figure holding a pair of scales and representing justice.

3. ***Male Nude Walking, Facing Right.***

4. ***Allegory of "Sculpture"***, 1889.

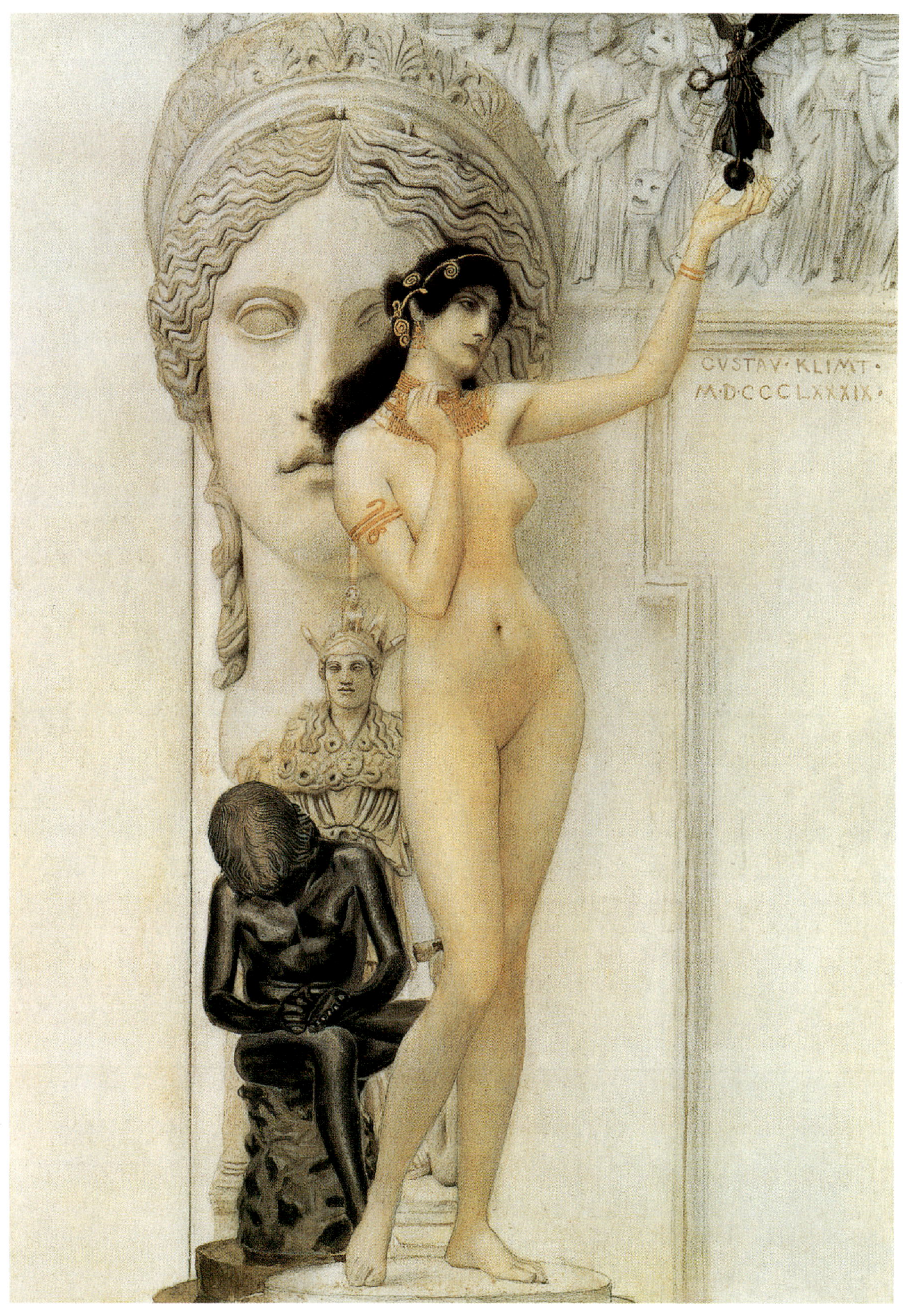
GVSTAV · KLIMT ·
M·D·CCCLXXXIX ·

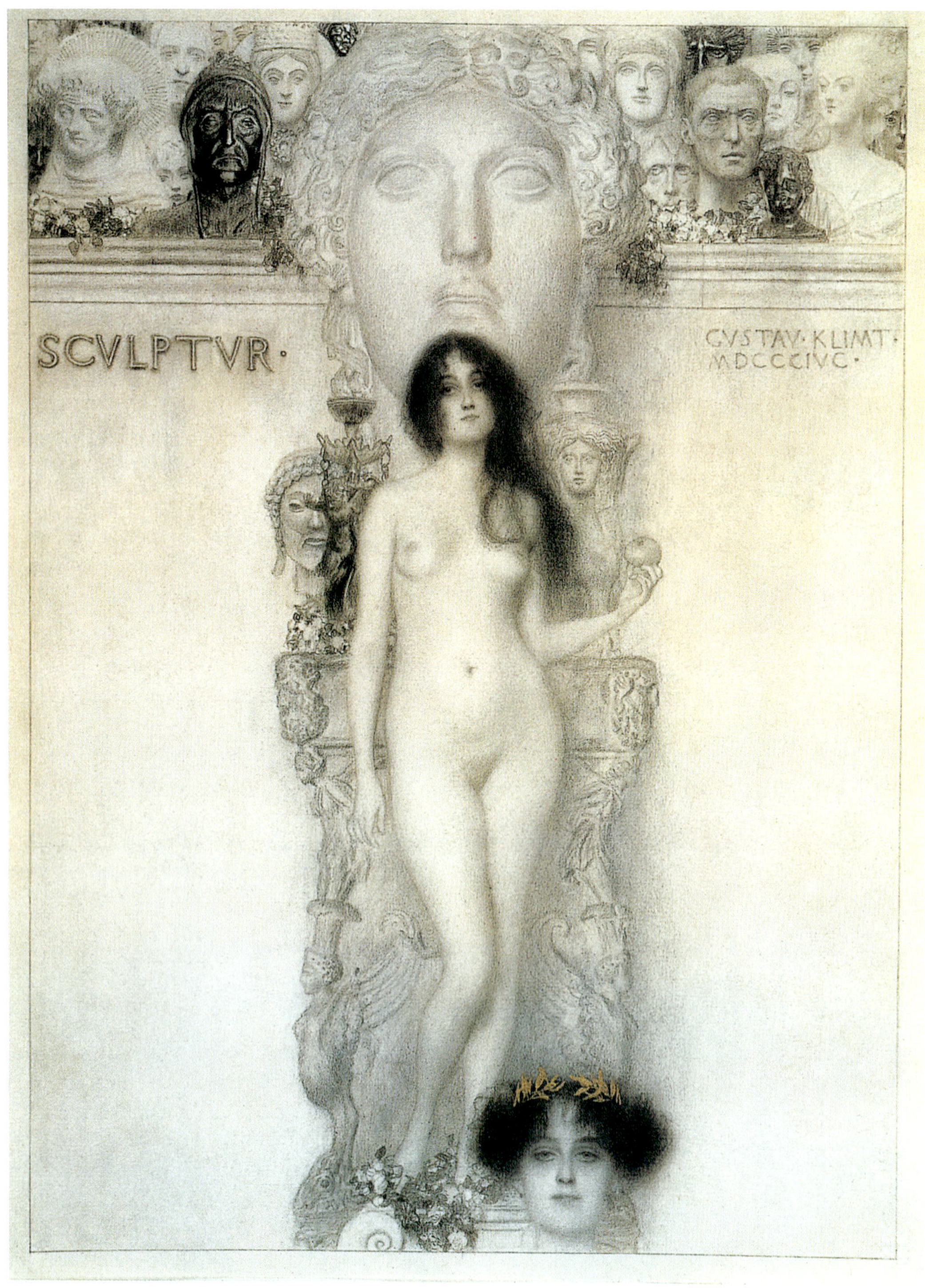
SCVLPTVR·
GVSTAV·KLIMT·
MDCCCIVC·

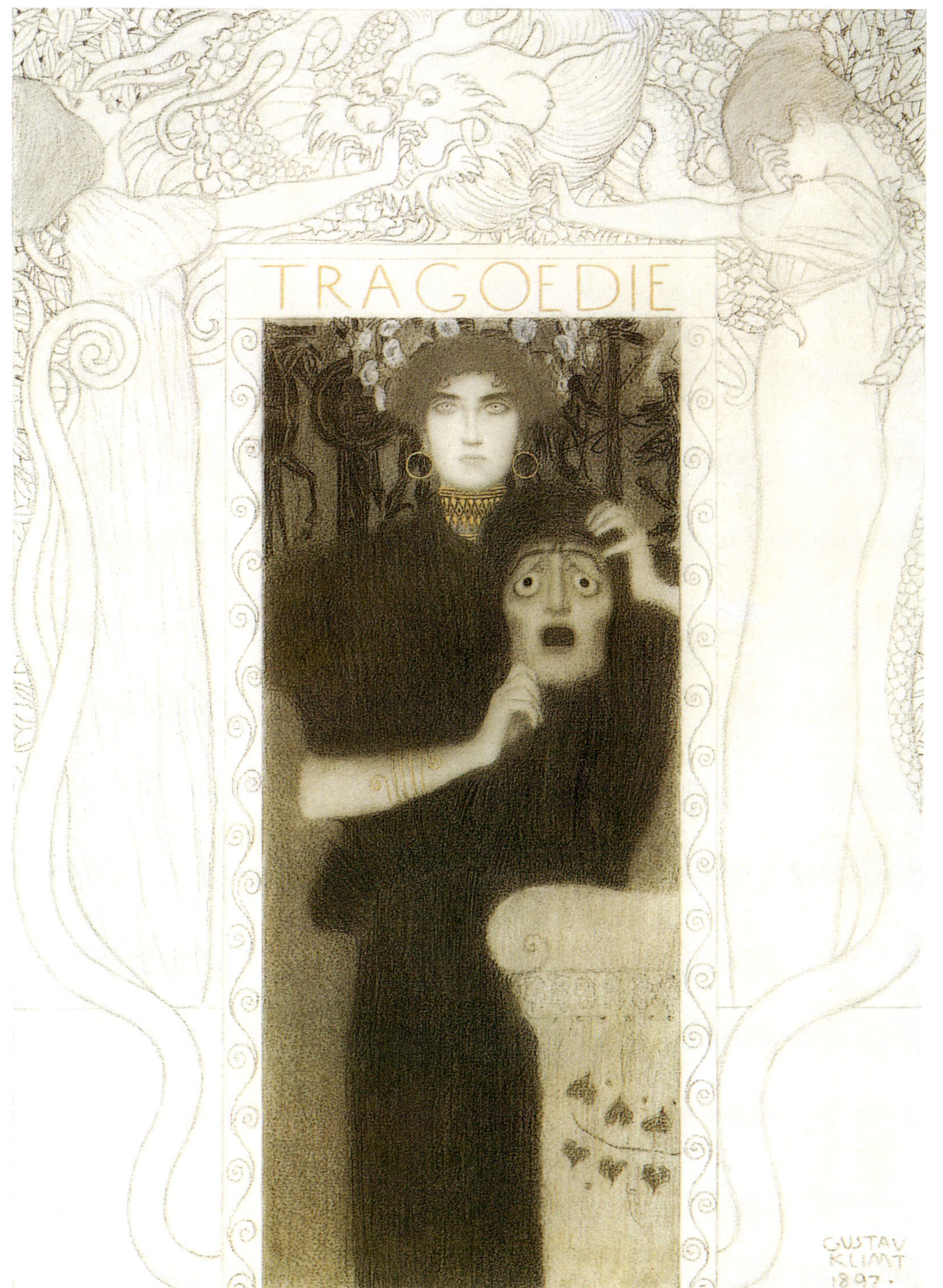

5. ***Final drawing for "Allegory of Sculpture"***, 1896.

6. ***Final drawing for the Allegory "Tragedy"***, 1897. Black chalk, wash, gold and white highlights, 42 x 31 cm, Vienna, Historisches Museum.

What they got, several years and much hard work later, caused such a scandal that Klimt eventually repaid the advances he had received and took the paintings back.

Despite the fact that on its first showing in Paris at the World Fair in 1900 *Philosophy* won him the gold medal, the Viennese were not of the same opinion as the French as to the painting's merits.

The first appearance of the unfinished *Medicine* in the following year caused even greater controversy. It is difficult to fathom precisely what Klimt meant to say about medicine in this painting.

The vision is chaotic, almost hellish. Its skulls, wrinkled elderly figures and mass of human bodies speak of human suffering, not of its cure. The viewer's eyes are drawn inevitably to the two striking female figures at the bottom and top left of the painting.

Clearly the figure at the bottom represents Medicine itself - the traditional symbol of the serpent suggests this - but this art nouveau woman, enlaced in gold ornament, looks more like a priestess likely to sacrifice a sick person than to heal them.

The naked woman at the top of the picture is remarkable for the dynamic abandonment of her pose. Our eyes are inevitably drawn to the woman's groin as she flings out her arms in a parody of crucifixion.

The sketch for the figure shows very clearly how bold and excellent a draughtsman Klimt was: the heavy line and subtle shading lead our eyes firmly to the woman's pubic hair.

Interestingly though, in the sketch the woman looks as if she might have posed lying down or leaning against something, whereas in the painting she is standing precariously unsupported, as if about to fall.

Both these and the other female figures around them represent a complete departure from the rotund, comfortable women of the traditional nineteenth-century academic style.

7. ***Athena Pallas***, 1898.
Oil on canvas,
75 x 75 cm, Vienna,
Historisches Museum.

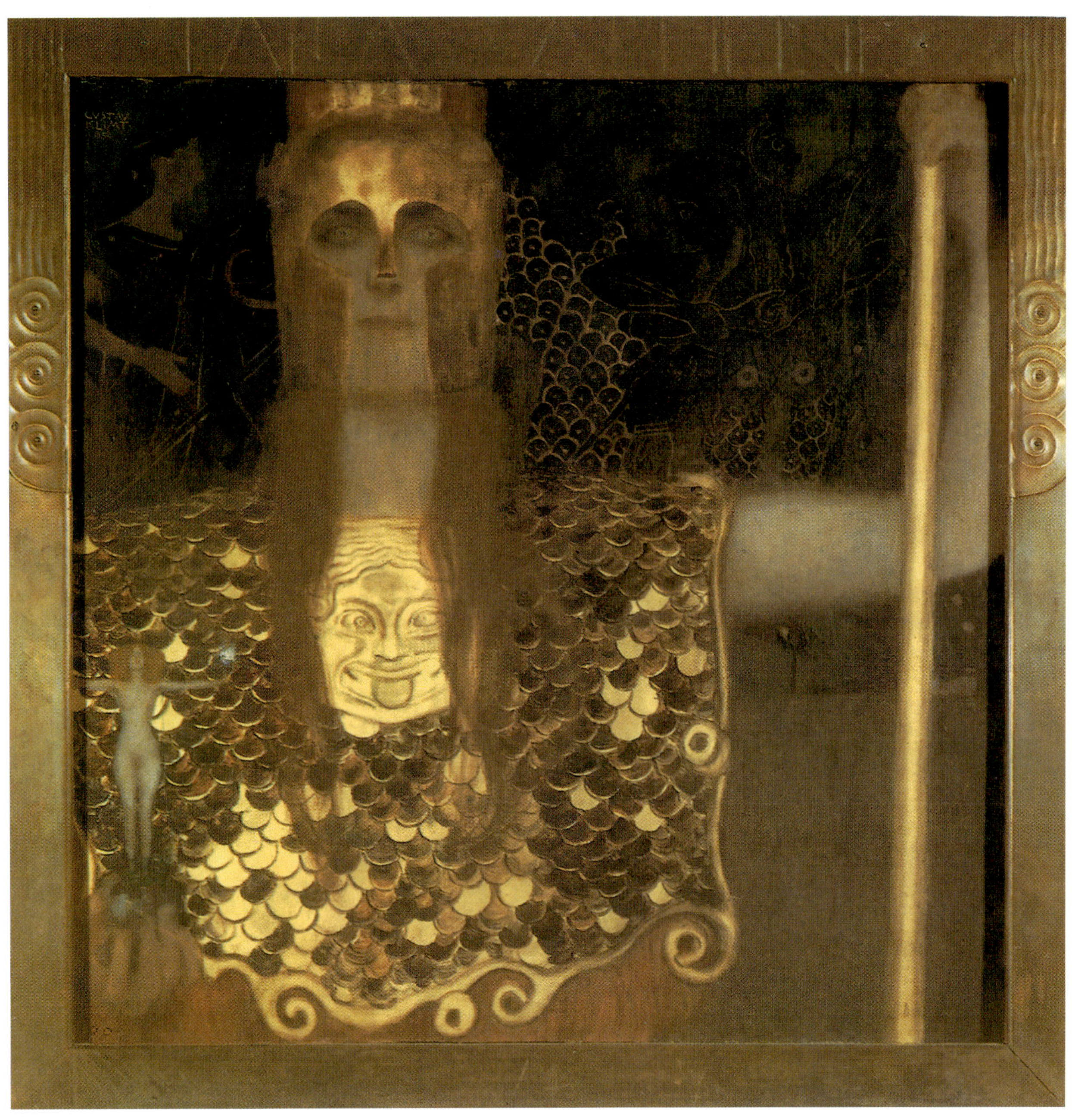

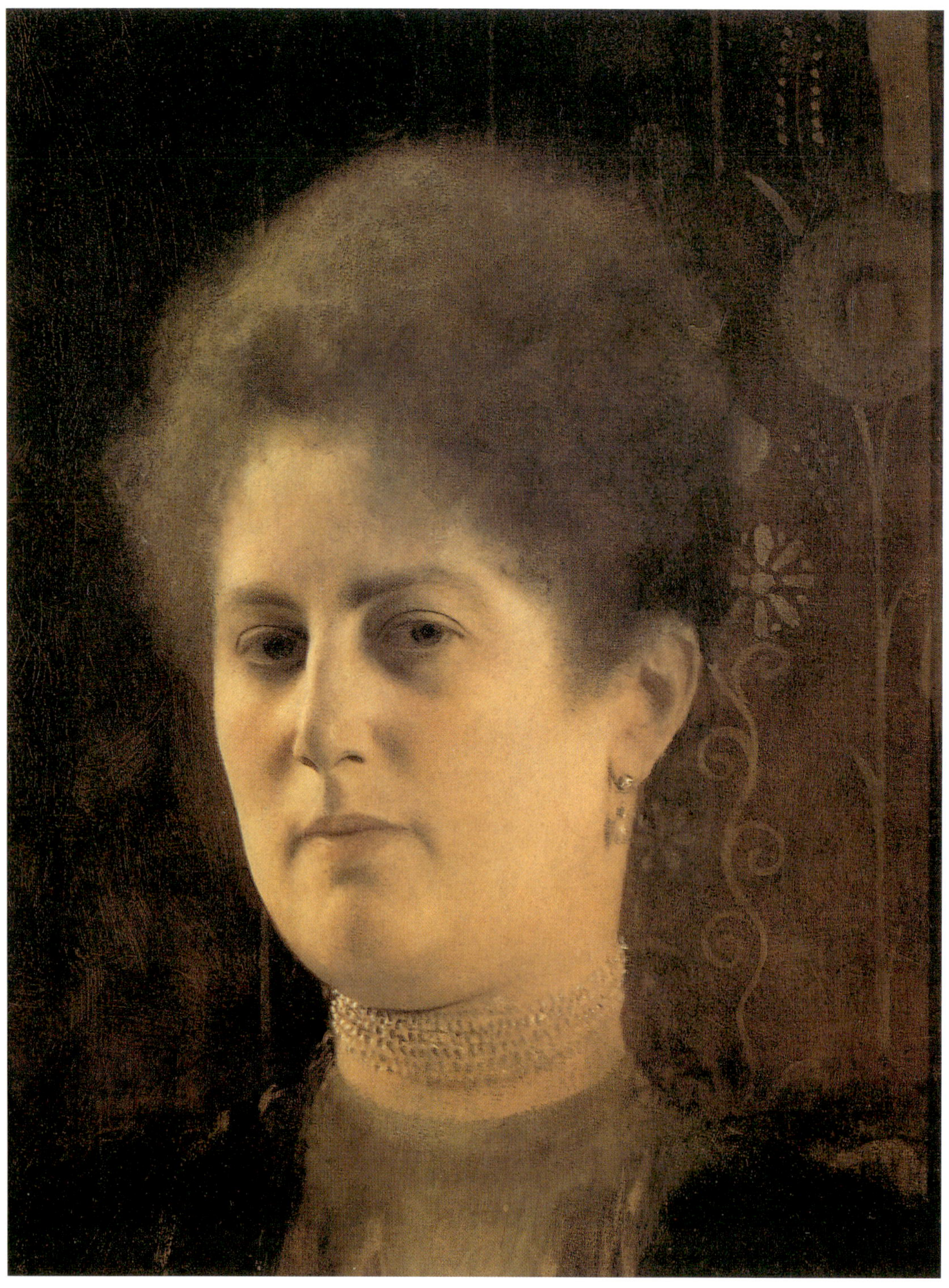

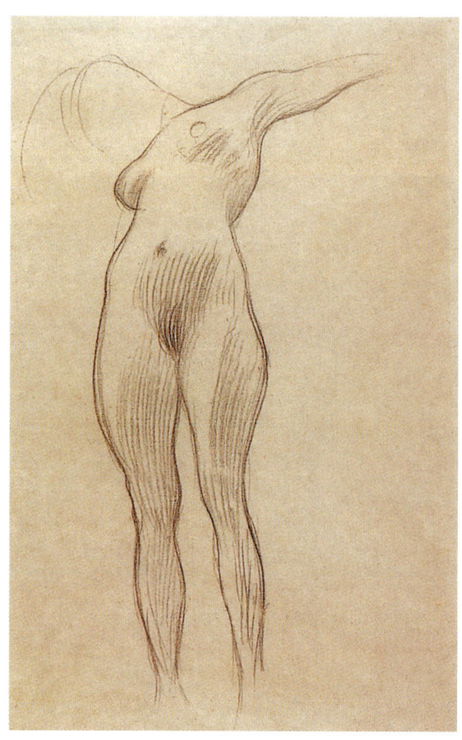

Klimt's women are long-haired, slender, lithe, and possess a sexual awareness that is both alluring and almost threatening in its directness.

Klimt's contemporary Berta Zuckerkandl makes the following comment in her memoirs: "Klimt had created from Viennese women an ideal female type: modern, with a boyish figure.

They had a mysterious fascination; although the word 'vamp' was still unknown he drew women with the fascination of a Greta Garbo or a Marlene Dietrich long before they actually existed." (*Ich erlebte fünfzig Jahre Weltgeschichte (I witnessed fifty years of world history)* Stockholm 1939.) Looking at his 1909 portrait *Woman in a Hat with Feather Boa* (p. 21) it is easy to see the truth of this statement.

8. ***Portrait of a woman (Mrs. Heymann?),*** about 1894. Oil on wood, 39 x 23 cm, Vienna, Historisches Museum.

9. ***Floating woman***, 1900. Study for "*Medicine*". Drawing 41.5x27.3 cm, Vienna, Graphische Sammlung Albertina.

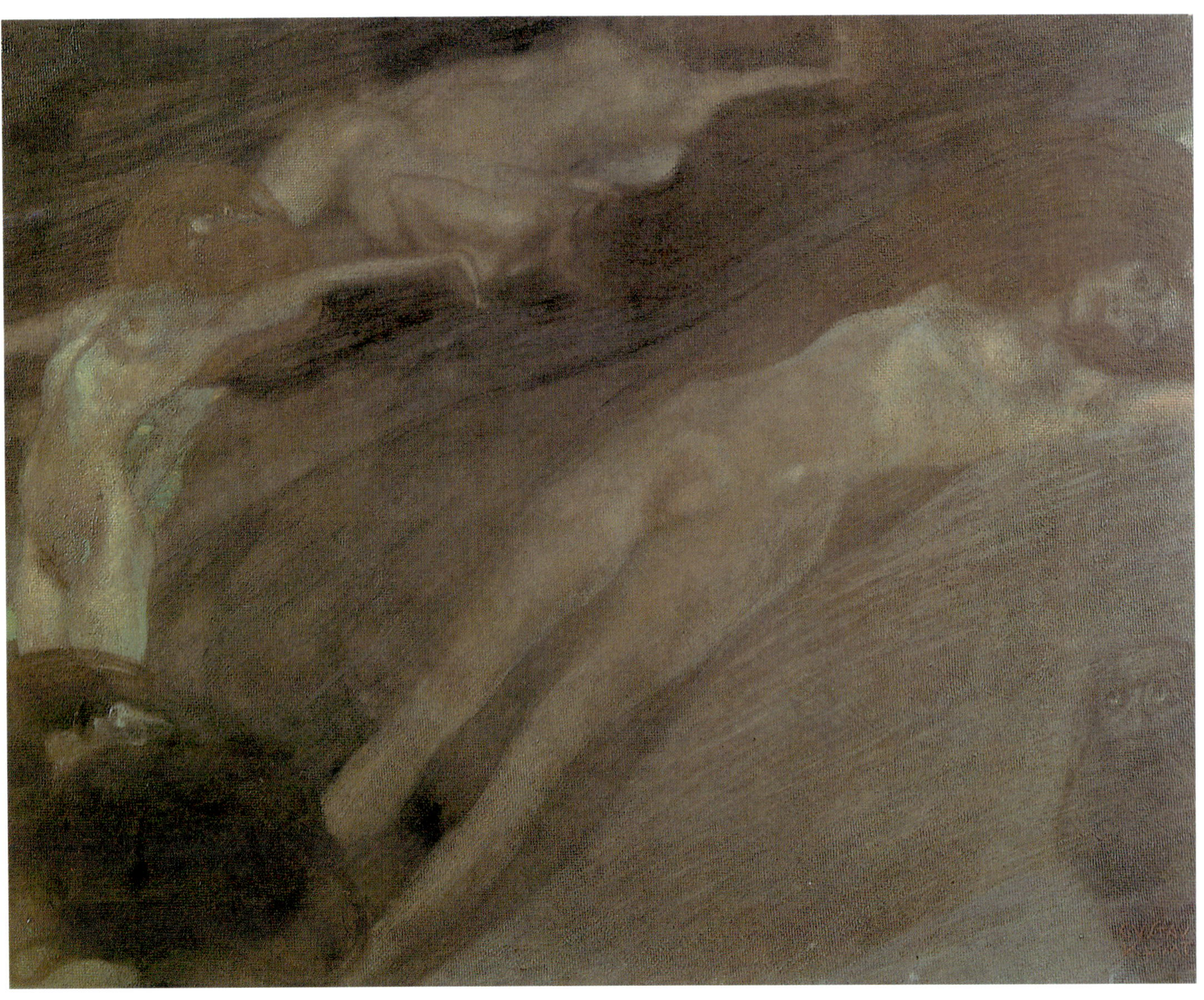

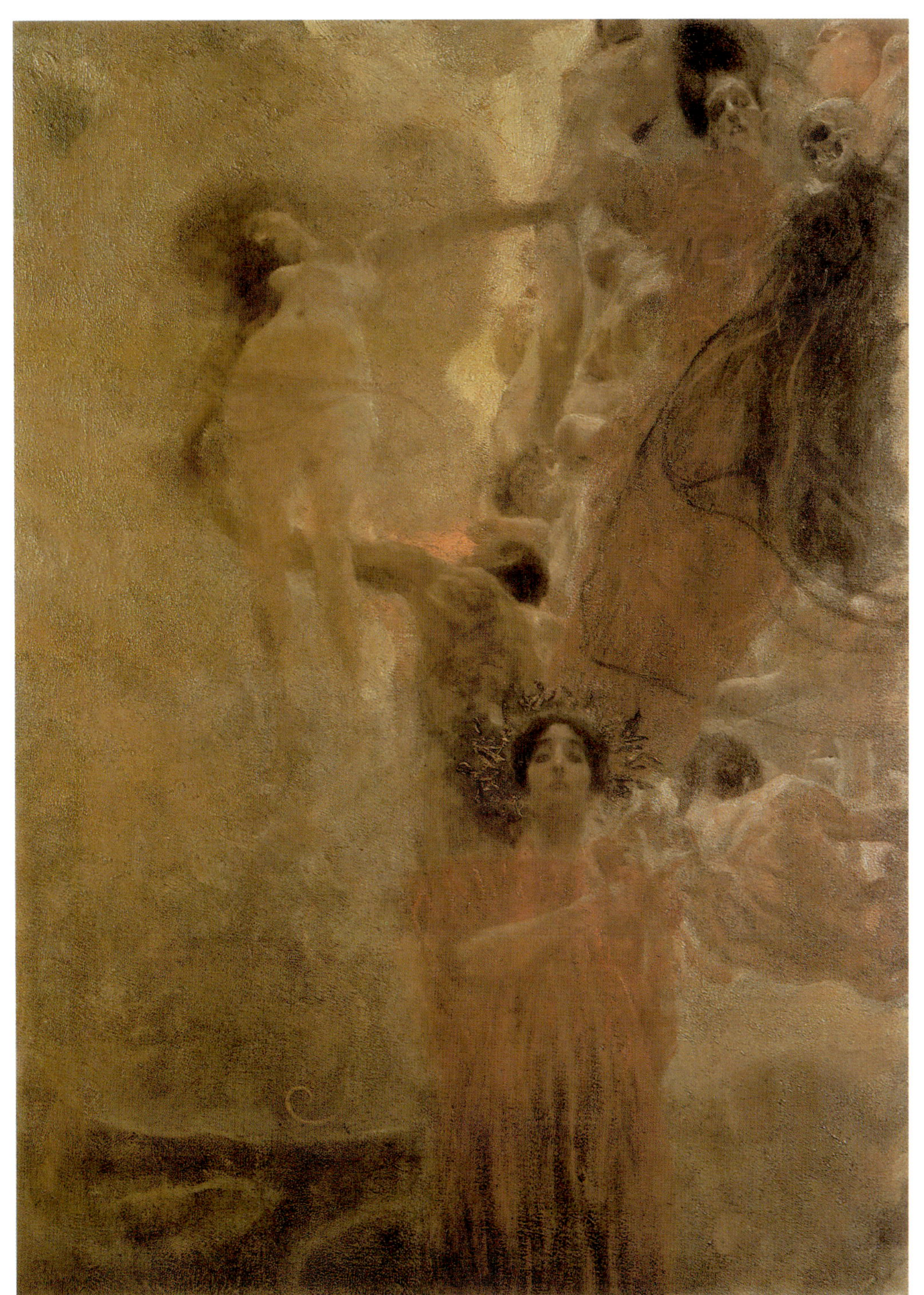

10. ***Flowing Water***, 1898. Oil on canvas, 52 x 65 cm, Private Collection.

11. ***Compositional project for "Medicine",*** 1897-1898. Graphite, 72 x 55 cm, Vienna.

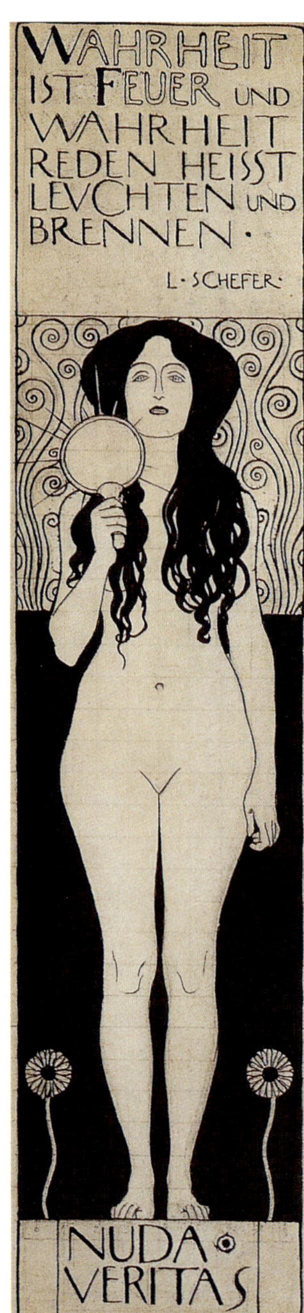

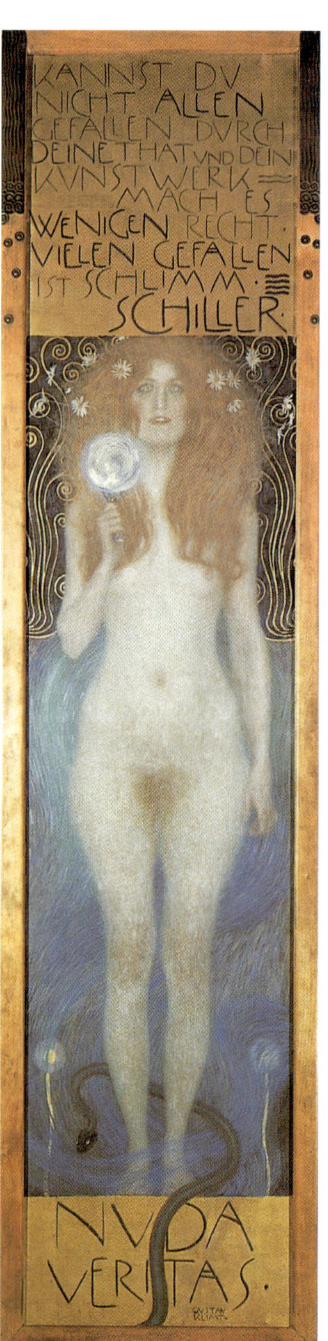

12. ***Final drawing for "Nuda Veritas"***, 1898.

13. ***Nuda Veritas***, 1899. Oil on canvas, 252 x 56 cm, Vienna.

14. ***Nuda Veritas (Detail)***, 1899. Oil on canvas, 252 x 56 cm, Vienna.

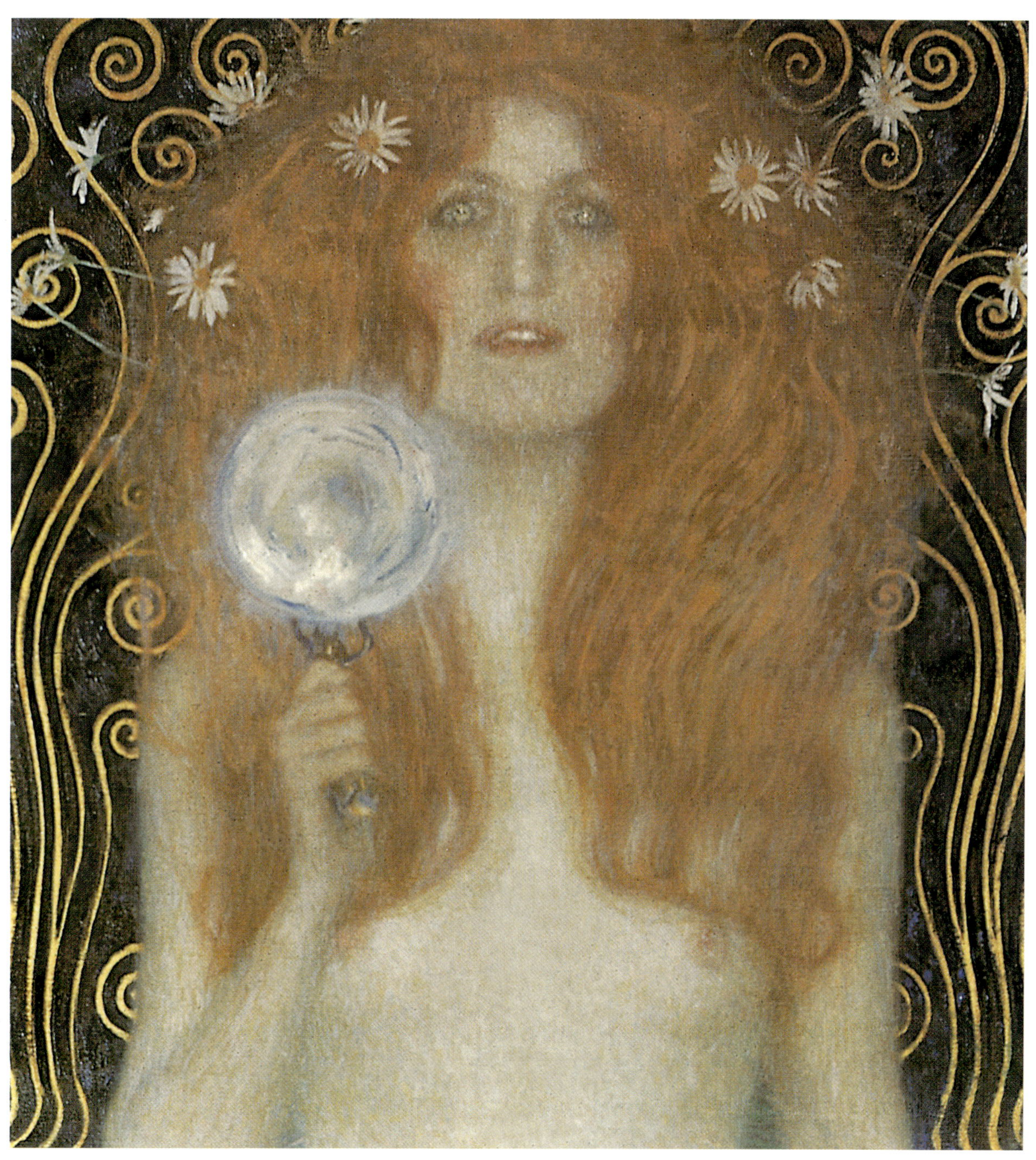

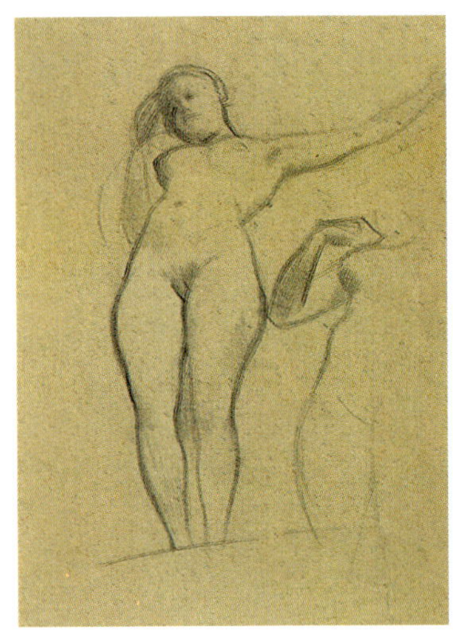

The woman's face, half-hidden by feathers and hat, looks not unlike a dark-haired version of Marilyn Monroe. The seductively half-closed eyes certainly echo many Monroe poses.

The Secession's fourteenth exhibition in 1902 led to yet another scandal. The exhibition centred around Max Klinger's statue of Beethoven and Klimt had decided to contribute a frieze.

The detail shown depicts *Lust, Lechery and Excess* (p. 26, 27), three allegorical figures designed to occupy part of the central wall of the room where Klinger's statue was exhibited.

Again, Klimt's purpose in choosing precisely these subjects for a tribute to Beethoven remains obscure, but they contain the seeds of many a later work, most notably the trademark use of exotically patterned textiles to form not so much a backdrop to the human figures but to create a composition of which pattern and human figure are equal parts.

In the figure of *Lust*, shown top left, Klimt uses the woman's hair both to hide her sex and to draw attention to it. The superb figure of *Excess* resembles not so much a woman as an oriental pasha, a man whose corpulence has reached such an extent that his chest has expanded to form female breasts.

Conservative Viennese society was once again profoundly shocked by these images, much in the same way that modern-day exhibition-goers are shocked by a Damien Hirst.

Klimt's contemporary Felix Salten relates: "Suddenly an exclamation came from the centre of the room: 'Hideous!' An aristocrat, a patron and collector, whom the Secession had let in today together with other close friends, had lost his temper at the sight of the Klimt frescoes.

He shouted the word in a high, shrill, sharp voice... he threw it up the walls like a stone. 'Hideous!'" Klimt's only response to this, as he worked away on the scaffolding above, was an amused glance in the direction of the departed man. This calm response perhaps best typifies Klimt's reaction to the scandals he caused.

15. ***Two studies of standing nude for the composition "Medicine".***

16. ***Woman in Hat with Feather Boa.***
1909, Oil on canvas,
69x55.8 cm,
Private Collection.

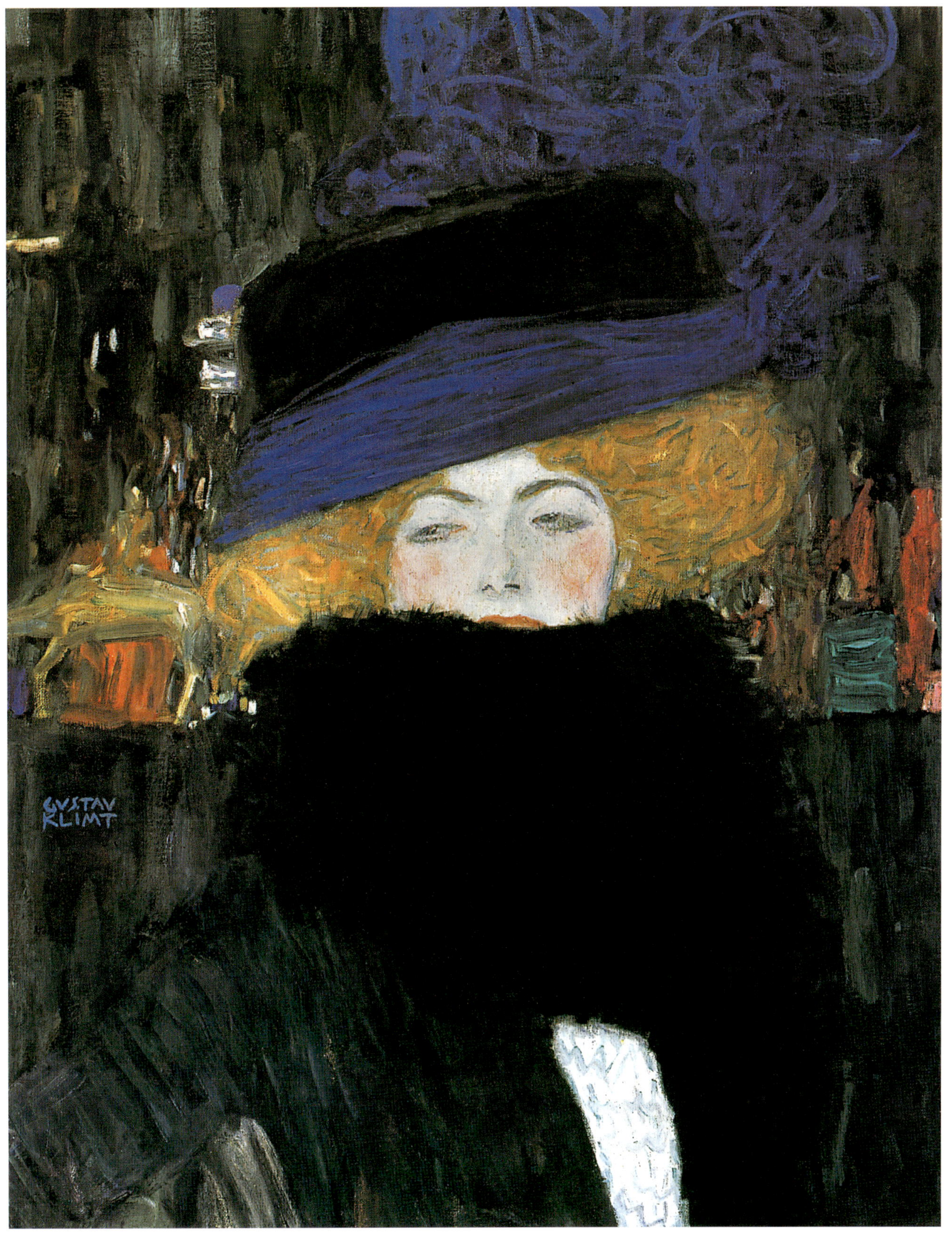
GUSTAV
KLIMT

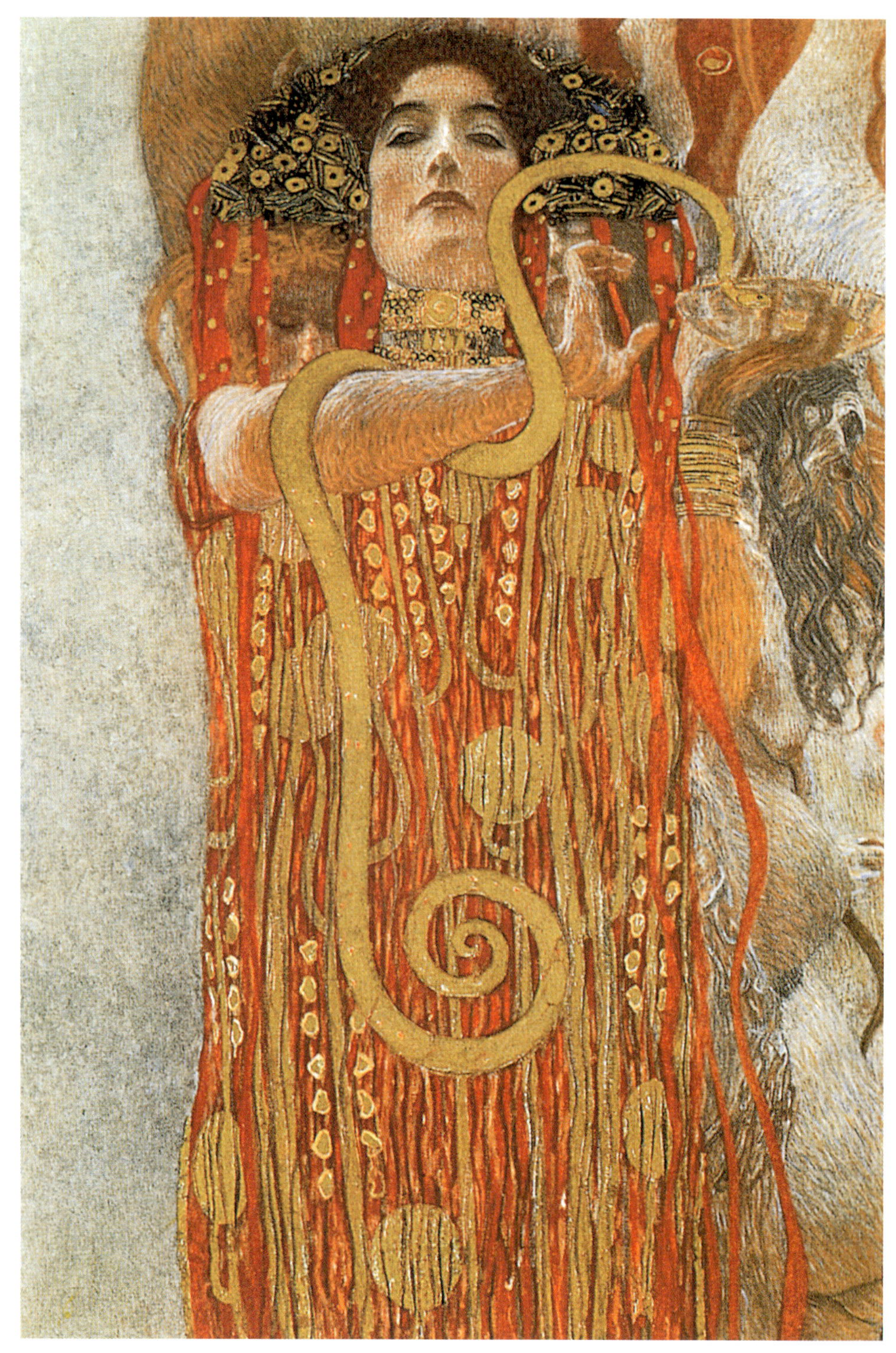

17. ***Medicine.***

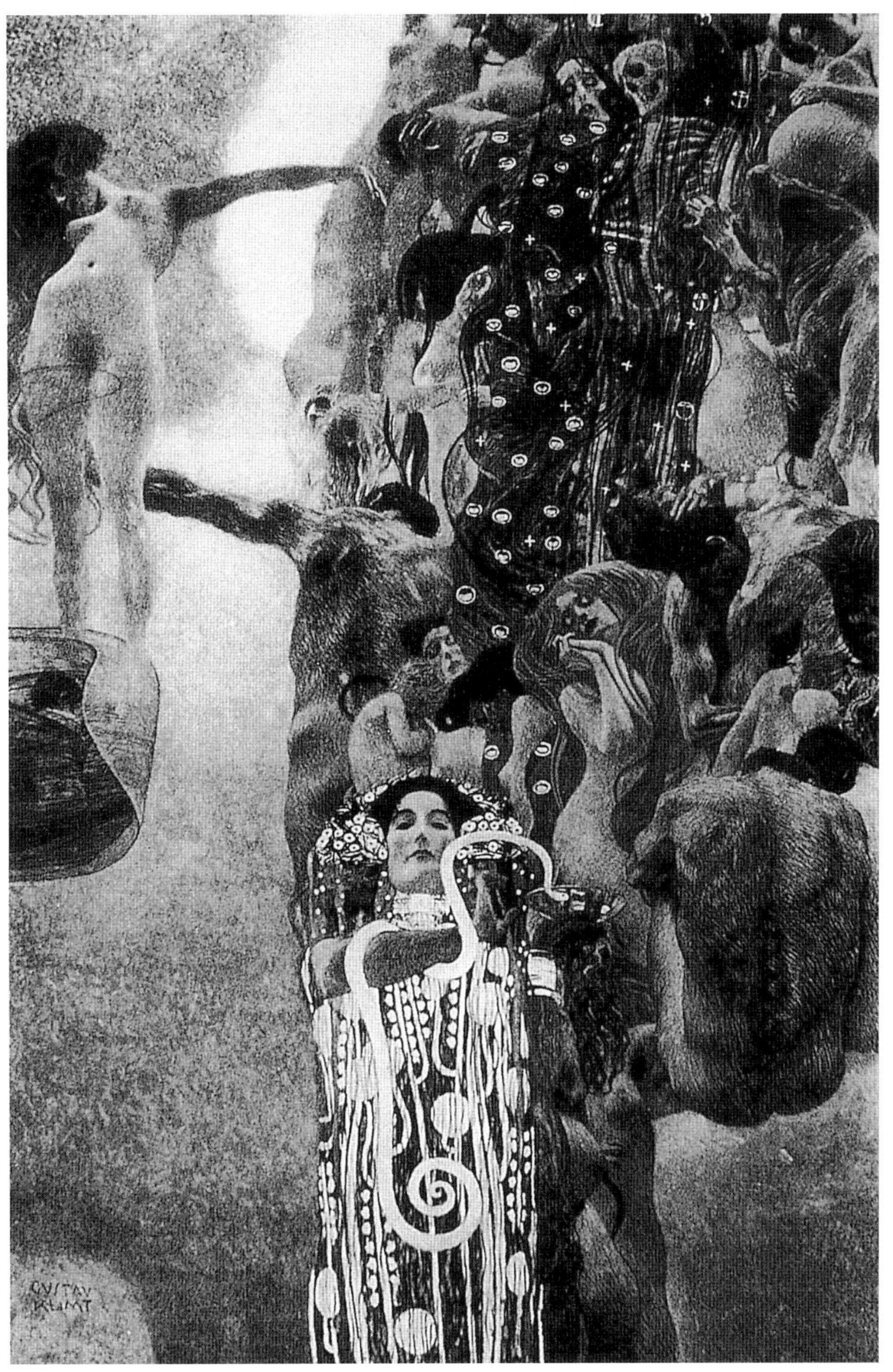

18. ***Medicine.***

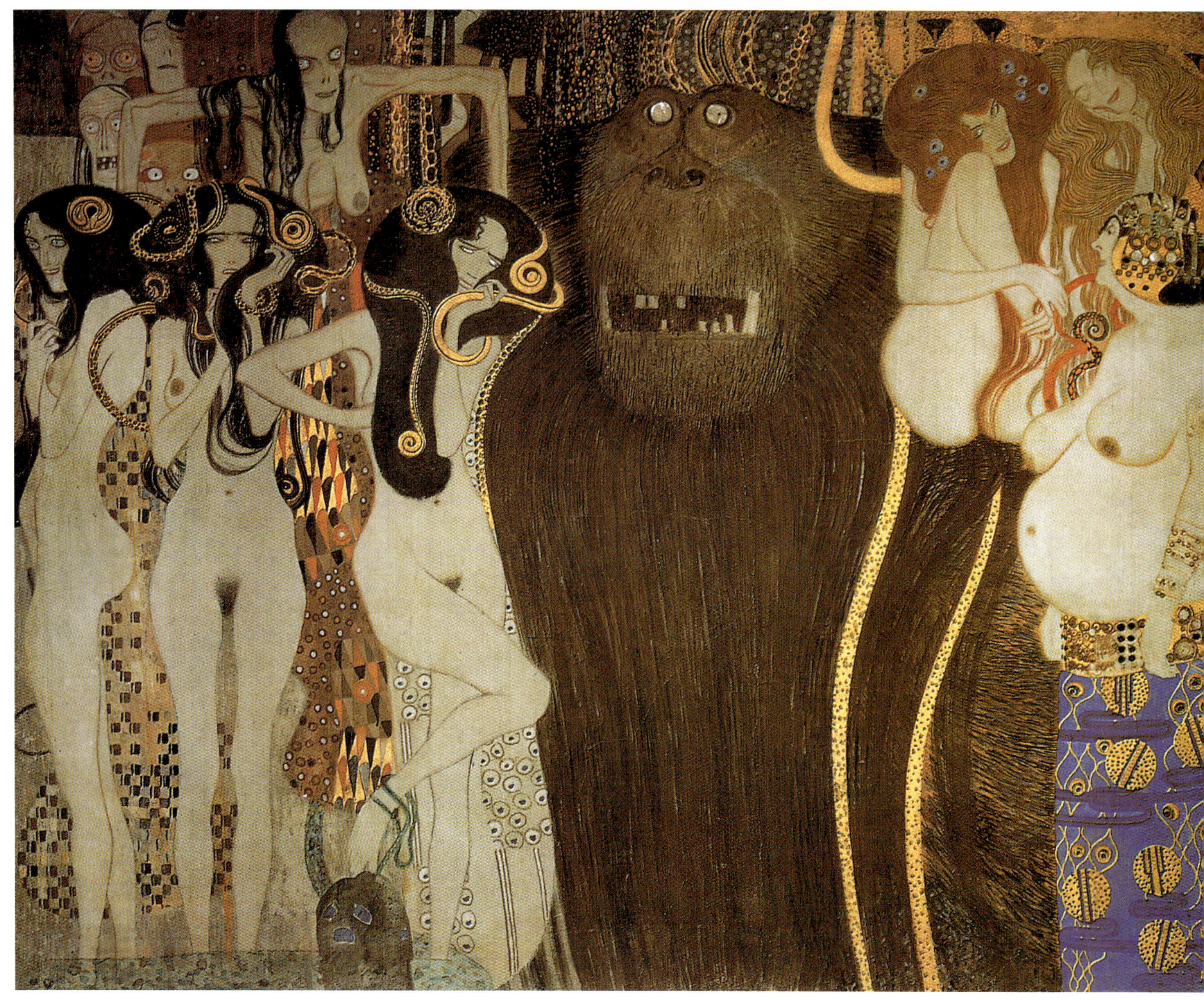

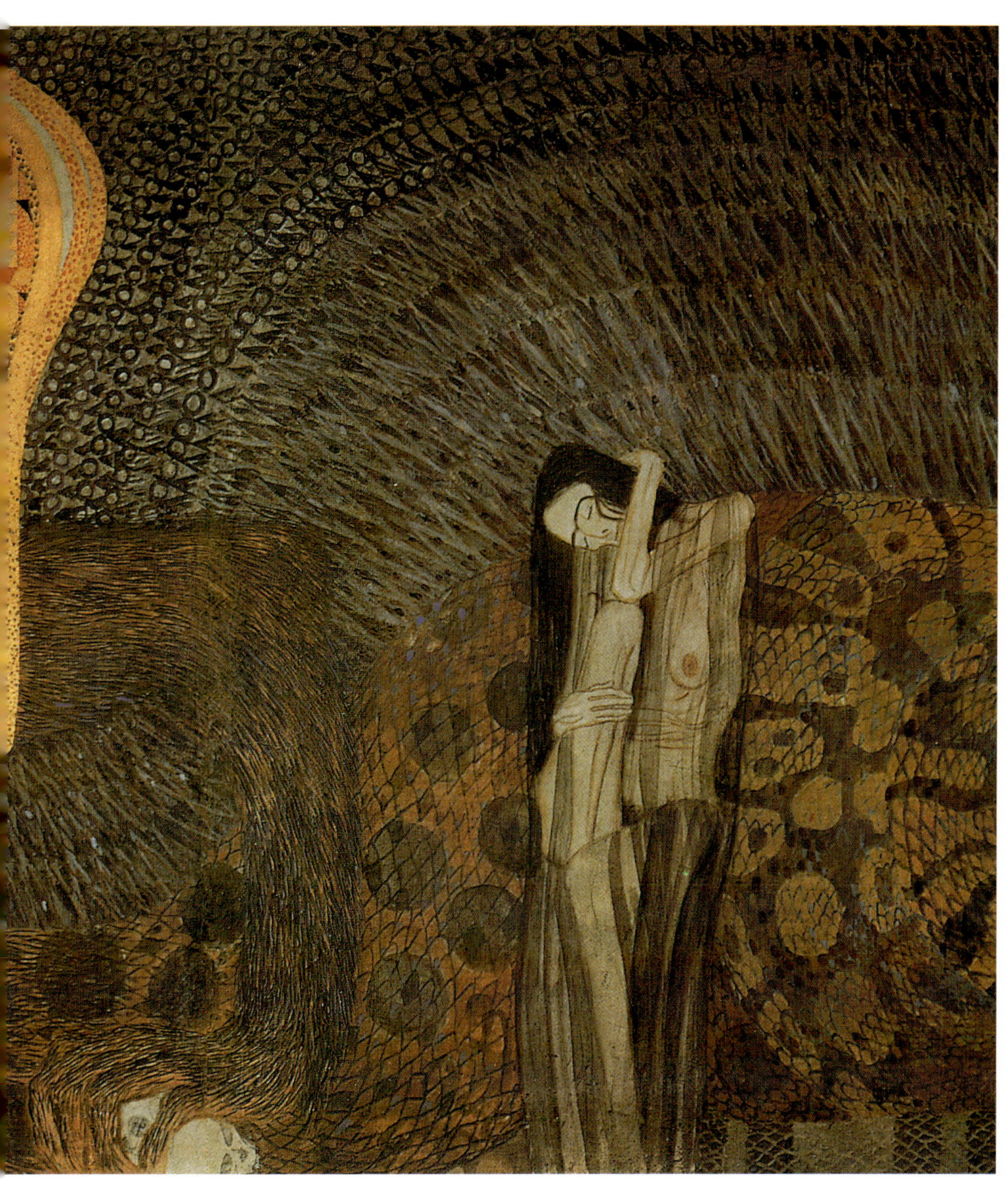

19. ***The Beethoven-Frieze (Detail)***, 1902. Casein on plaster, H. 220 cm, Vienna, Österreichische Galerie.

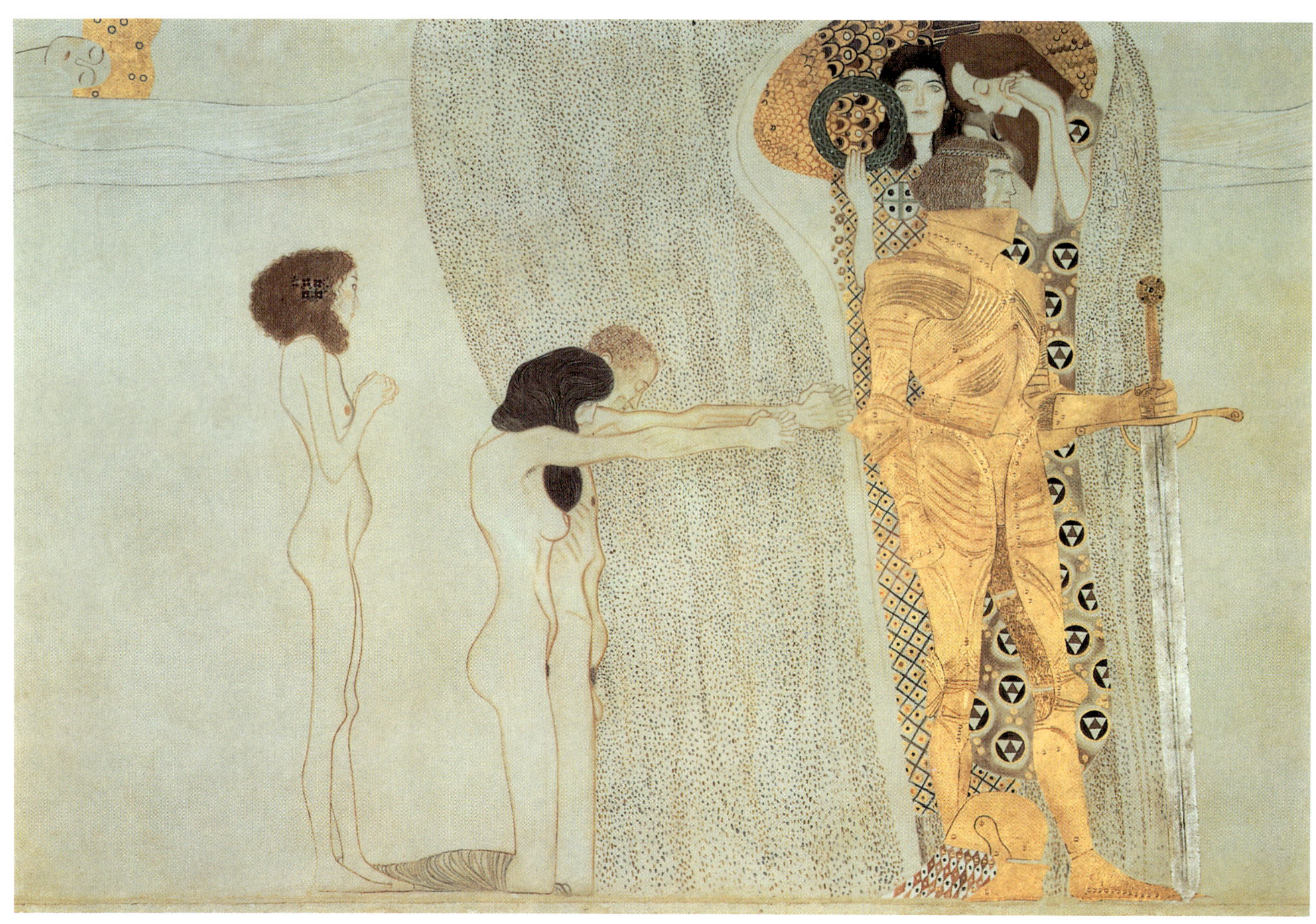

20. ***The Beethoven-Frieze (Detail),*** 1902.

21. ***The Beethoven-Frieze (Detail),*** 1902.

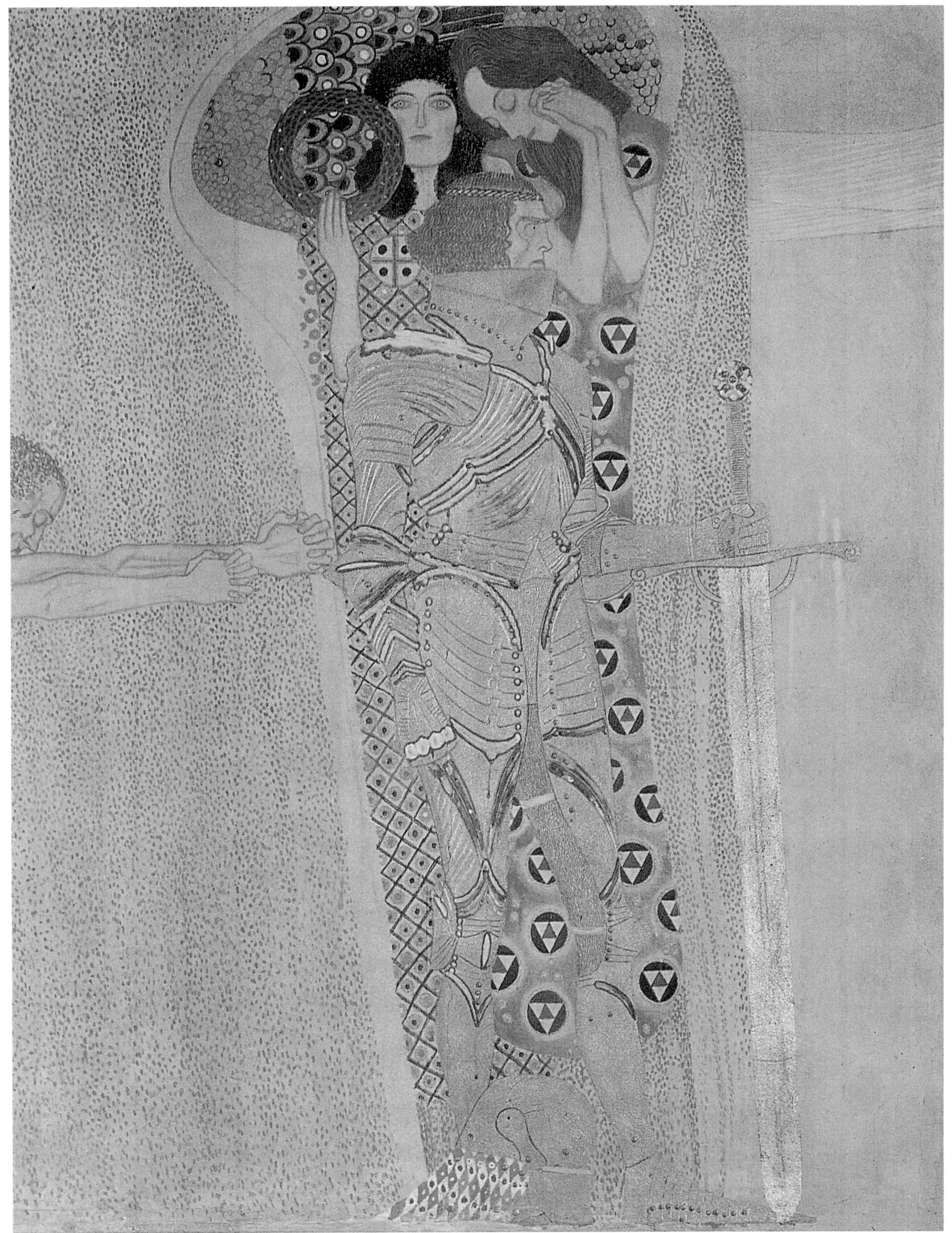

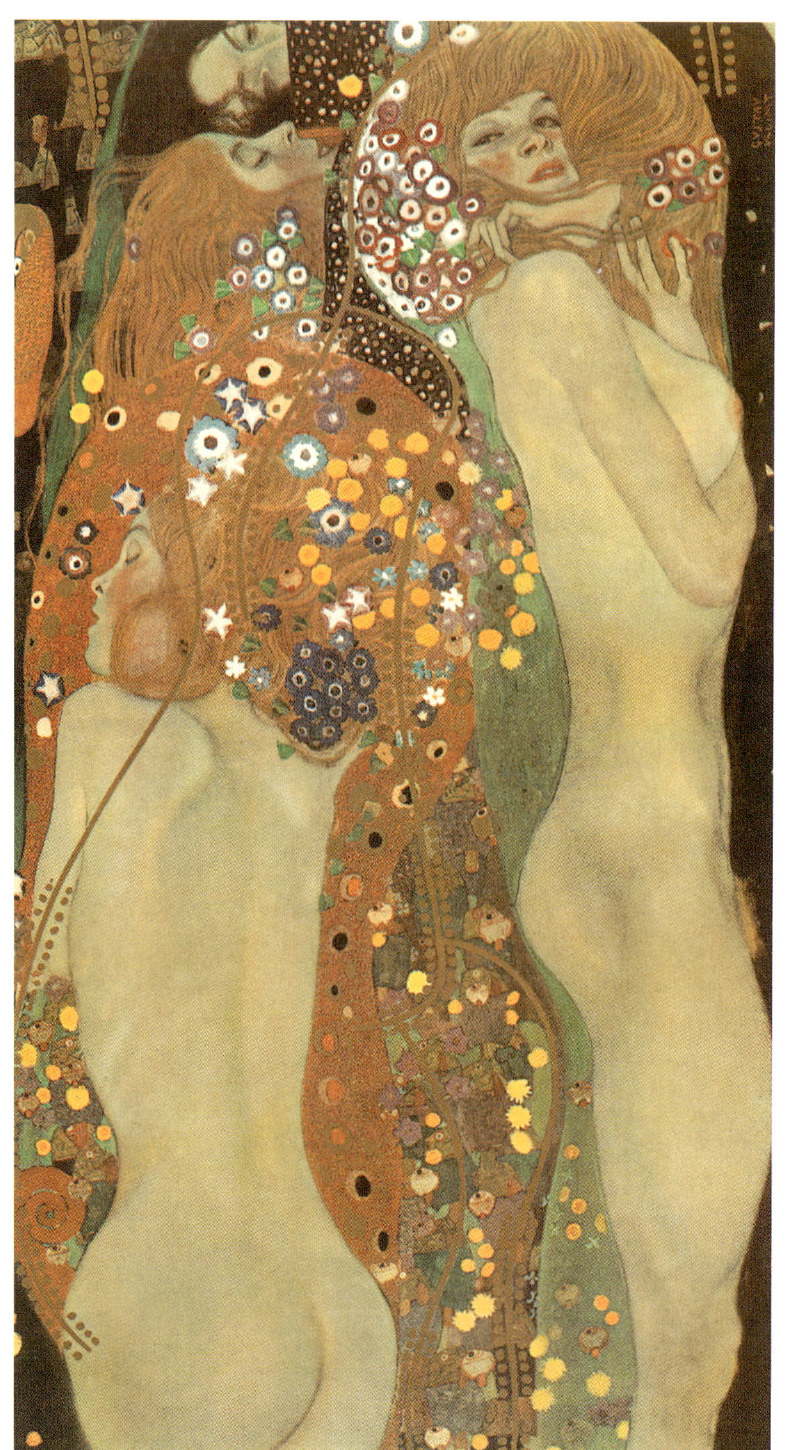

22. ***Water Snakes II***, 1904-1907. Oil on canvas, 80 x 145 cm, Private Collection.

23. ***The Three Ages of Women.*** 1905,Galleria Nazionale d' Arte Moderna, Roma.

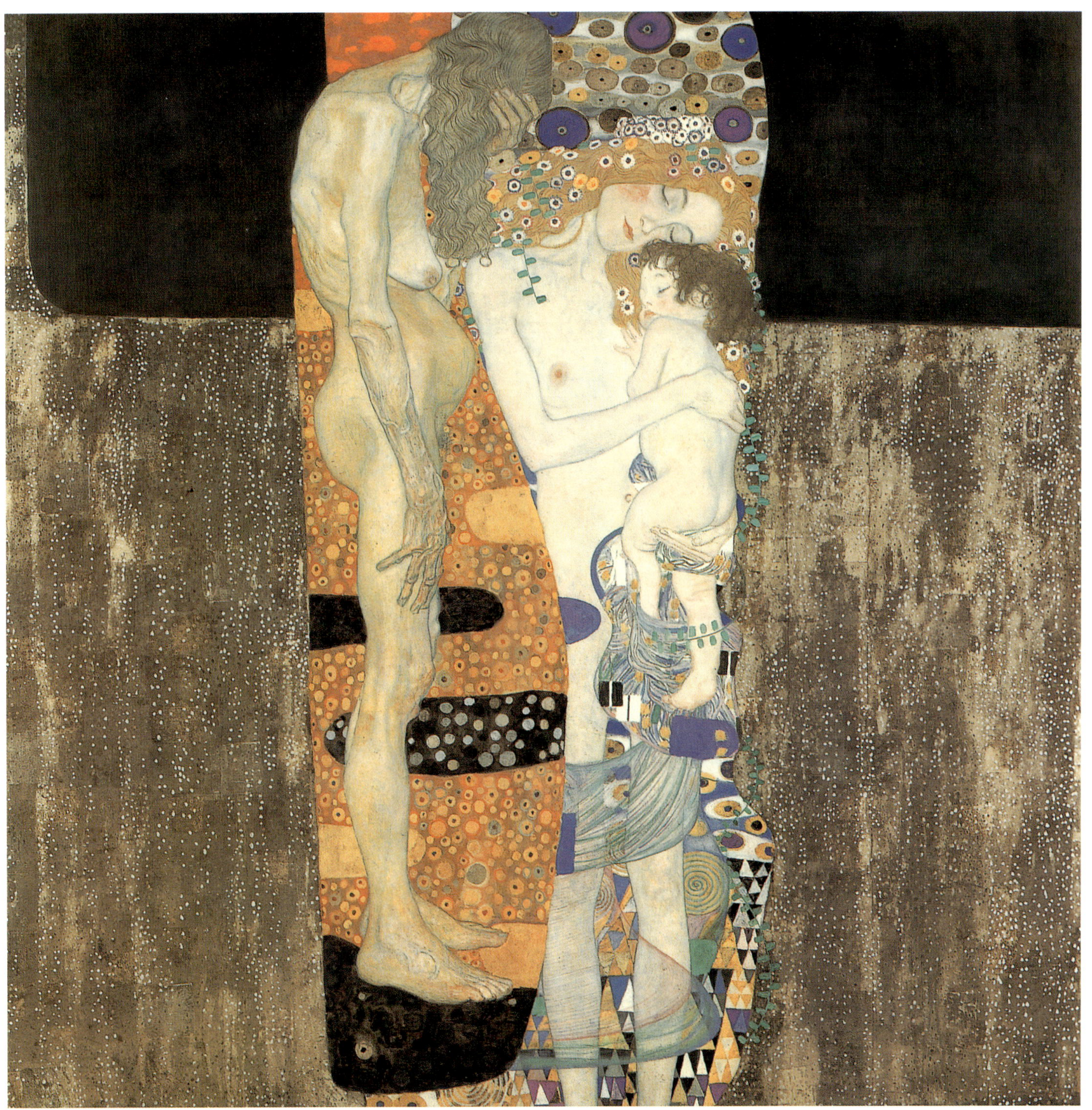

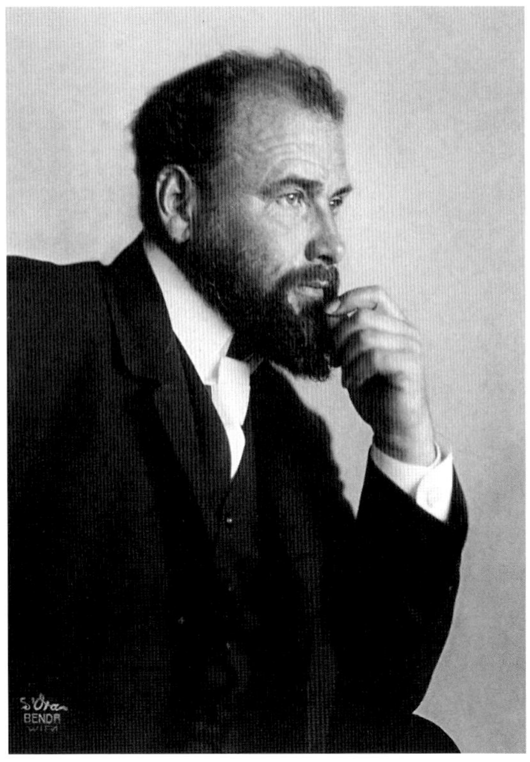

24. ***Gustav Klimt***, Photo.

Although the faculty paintings ensured that Klimt swiftly lost the patronage of the Emperor and other establishment figures, he was fortunate enough to be able to earn an extremely comfortable living from painting portraits and thus did not have to worry about this loss.

Three times, however, he was refused a professorship of the Academy. Only in 1917 was he offered the small consolation of being made an honorary member.

Fin de siècle Vienna

It must be remembered that despite their tastes for balls, the opera, theatre and music, the Viennese upper classes were extremely conservative in their tastes.

A combination of strict Roman Catholicism and rigid social mores kept the them buttoned up, at least on the surface.

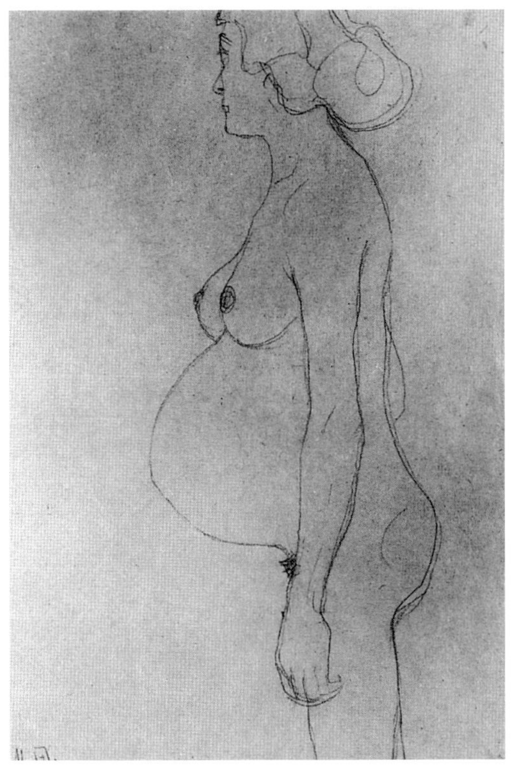

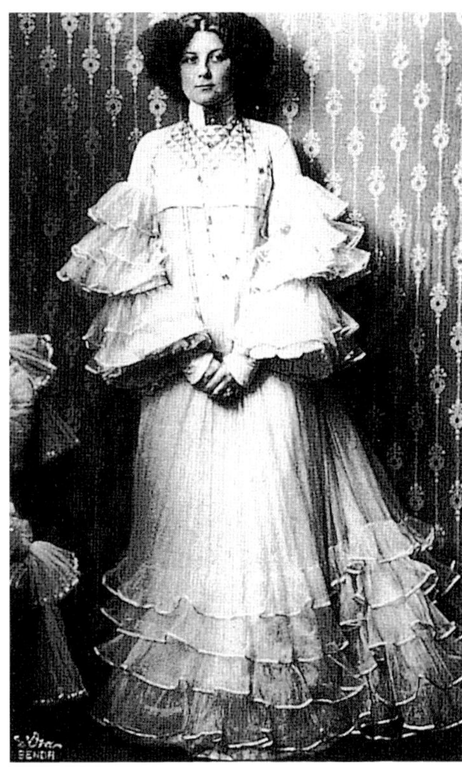

And whilst people were only too happy to indulge in all sorts of sensual pleasures that were sanctioned by society - the waltz, for example - they did not appreciate having openly erotic, ugly or sexual subjects thrust before them, a double standard which speaks volumes about the fin de siècle morality.

The Vienna into which Klimt was born was a city perched uncomfortably on the cusp of two eras. Then, it was still the capital of a far-reaching empire of over fifty million inhabitants, ruled by the Emperor Franz Joseph.

By the time of Klimt's death in 1918, the Habsburg Empire itself had only seven months left to live. Austria then became a tiny nation state of seven million inhabitants, three million of whom were concentrated around Vienna. Twenty years later it was absorbed by Nazi Germany under the leadership of Adolf Hitler, himself, ironically, born on Austrian soil.

25. ***Pregnant Nude, Standing, Left Profile, Study for "Hope II",*** 1907. Black chalk, 49 x 31 cm, Vienna, Historisches Museum.

26. ***Emilie Flöge,*** Photo.

27. ***Portrait of Emilie Flöge.***
1902, Oil on canvas, 181x84 cm, Historisches Museum des Stadt Wien, Vienna.

28. ***Hope I.***
1903,Oil on canvas.

29. ***Hope II.***
1907-1908, Oil, Gold and Platinum on canvas, 110.5x110.5 cm, Museum of Modern Art, New York.

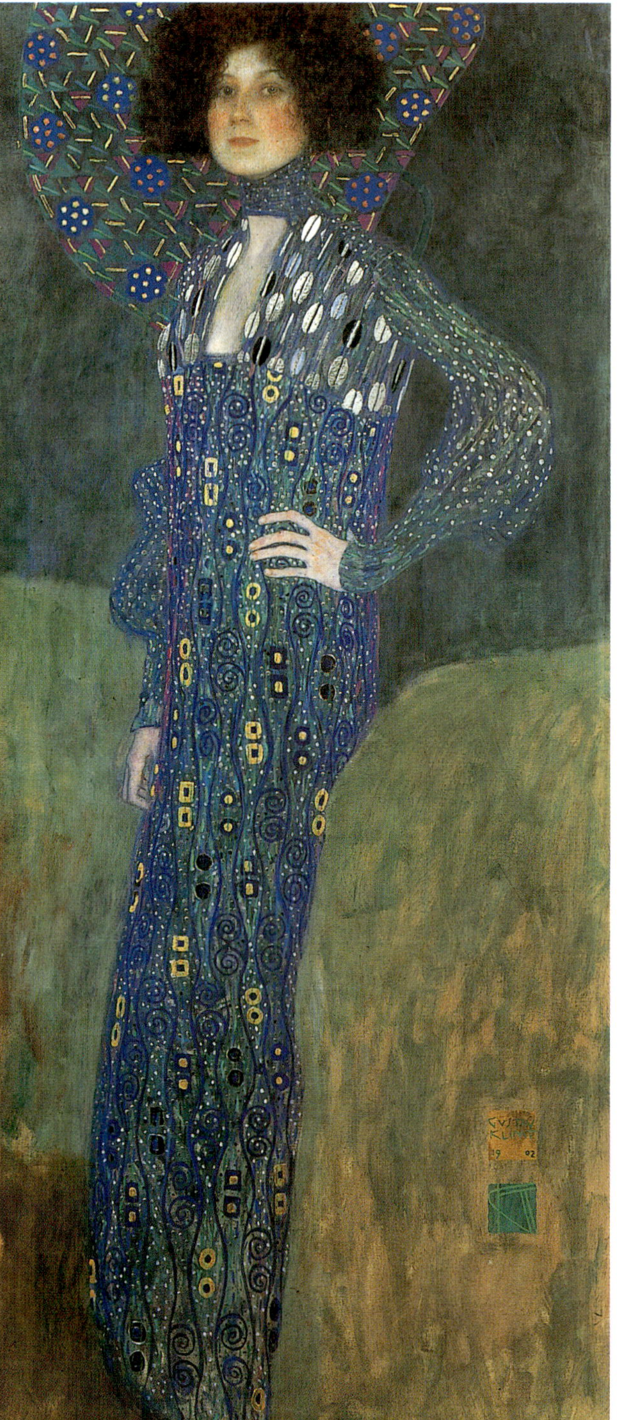

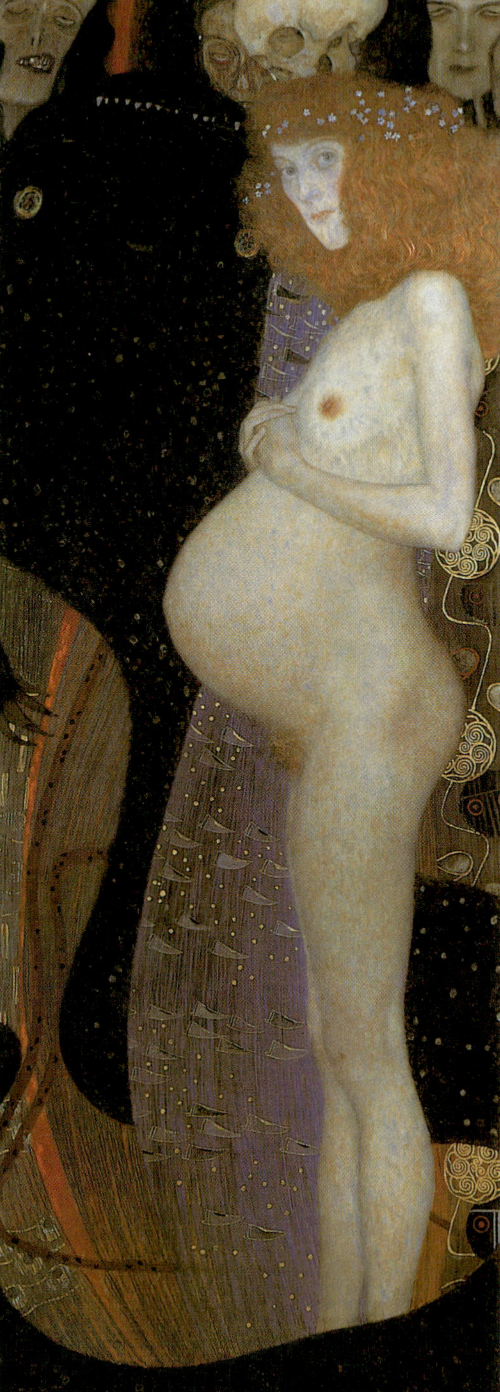

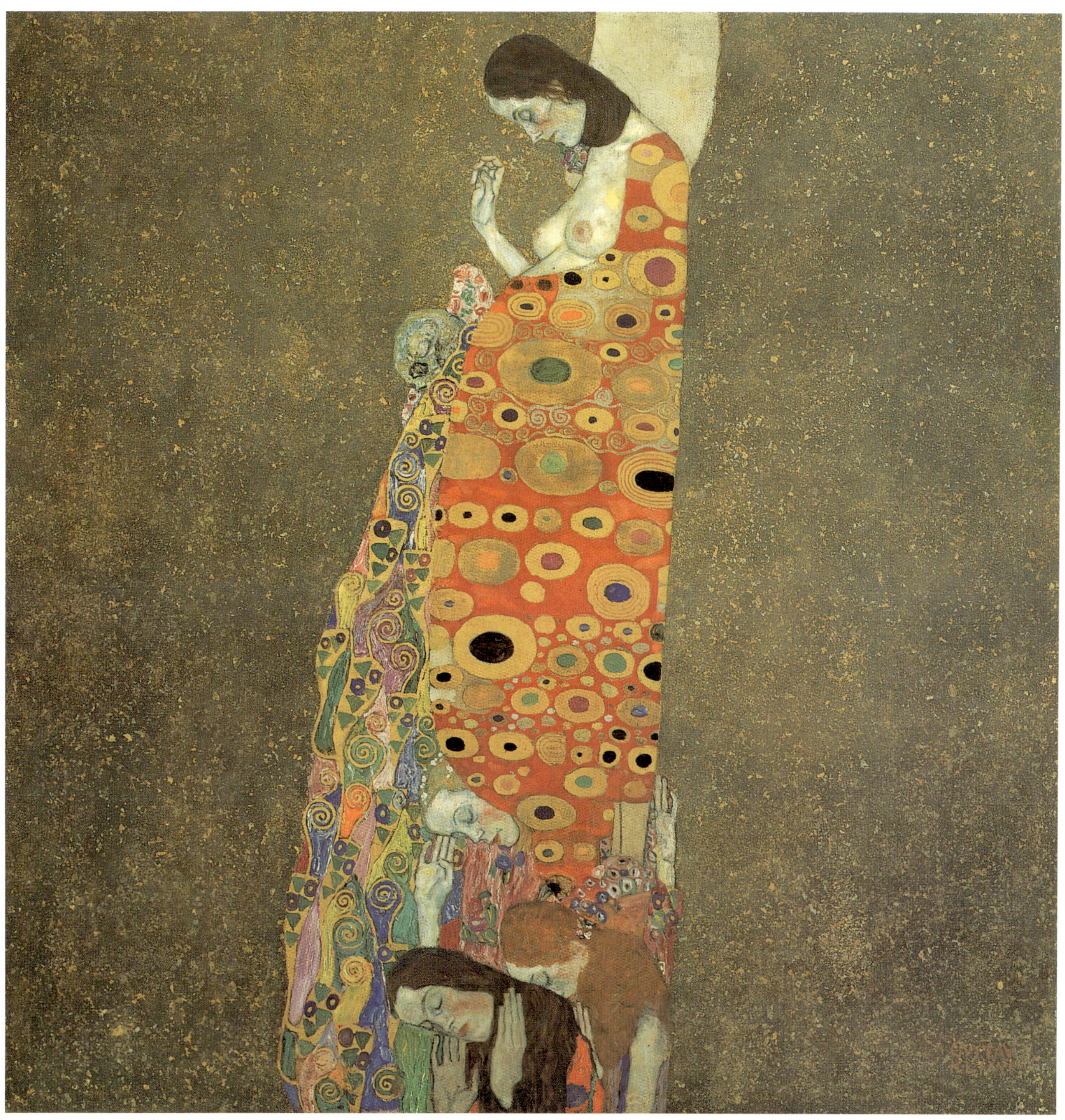

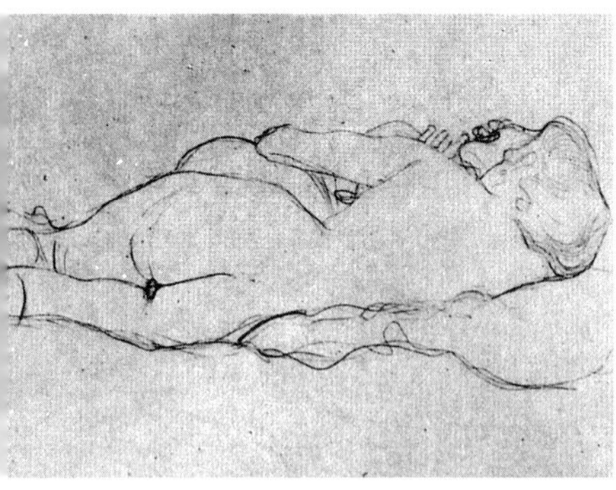

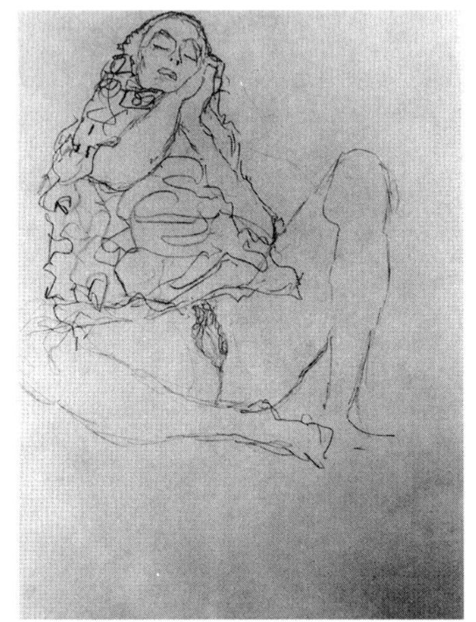

The period of decline had begun even before Klimt was born. Military defeats across the Empire sounded warning bells for future stability, whilst Vienna was filling up with Czechs, Gypsies, Hungarians, Poles, Jews, and Rumanians - immigrants from the poorest parts of the Empire, all in search of work, often living in appalling conditions.

The wealthy Viennese, however, chose not to acknowledge these signals of future trouble but rather to ignore the outside world and immerse themselves in a whirl of pleasurable activities.

This was a period of great musicians - Brahms, Bruckner, Strauss the younger, Schönberg, Mahler and, of course, Franz Lehàr, creator of the light operettas so beloved of the Viennese. It was also the era of Sigmund Freud, Alfred Adler, Arthur Schnitzler, and amidst all this, Klimt.

Lovers and Friends

It is one of the most tantalising facts about a man so well-known in times comparatively recent to our own that almost nothing concrete is known about Klimt's personal life, a fact largely due to his own reticence on the subject.

Whilst the facts of his artistic career are well-charted, knowledge of his private life depends entirely on hearsay. On the one hand, he is depicted as a ladies' man, built like a peasant, strong as an ox, sleeping with countless women, including all of his models.

On the other hand, he is seen as a hypochondriac and a confirmed bachelor of regular habits, living with his mother and sisters while keeping a studio in the suburbs to which he went to work regularly every day: "Klimt's daily routines were very bourgeois. He was so engrossed in them that any divergence from his normal course was a horror to him; going anywhere was a major event, and a big trip was only conceivable if his friends did all the shopping for him beforehand, down to the smallest detail." (Hans Tietze, *Gustav Klimts Persönlichkeit nach Mitteilungen seiner Freunde*, 1919)

30. ***Friends Embracing***, 1905. Graphite, 38 x 57 cm.

31. ***Nude seated with closed eyes***, 1913. Graphite, 57 x 37 cm, Vienna, Historisches Museum.

Klimt never married, but had a long relationship with Emilie Flöge, the sister of his brother Ernst's wife. In 1891, Ernst had married Helene Flöge, one of two sisters who ran a fashion house in Vienna. The marriage only lasted fifteen months, but through Helene Gustav had met Emilie.

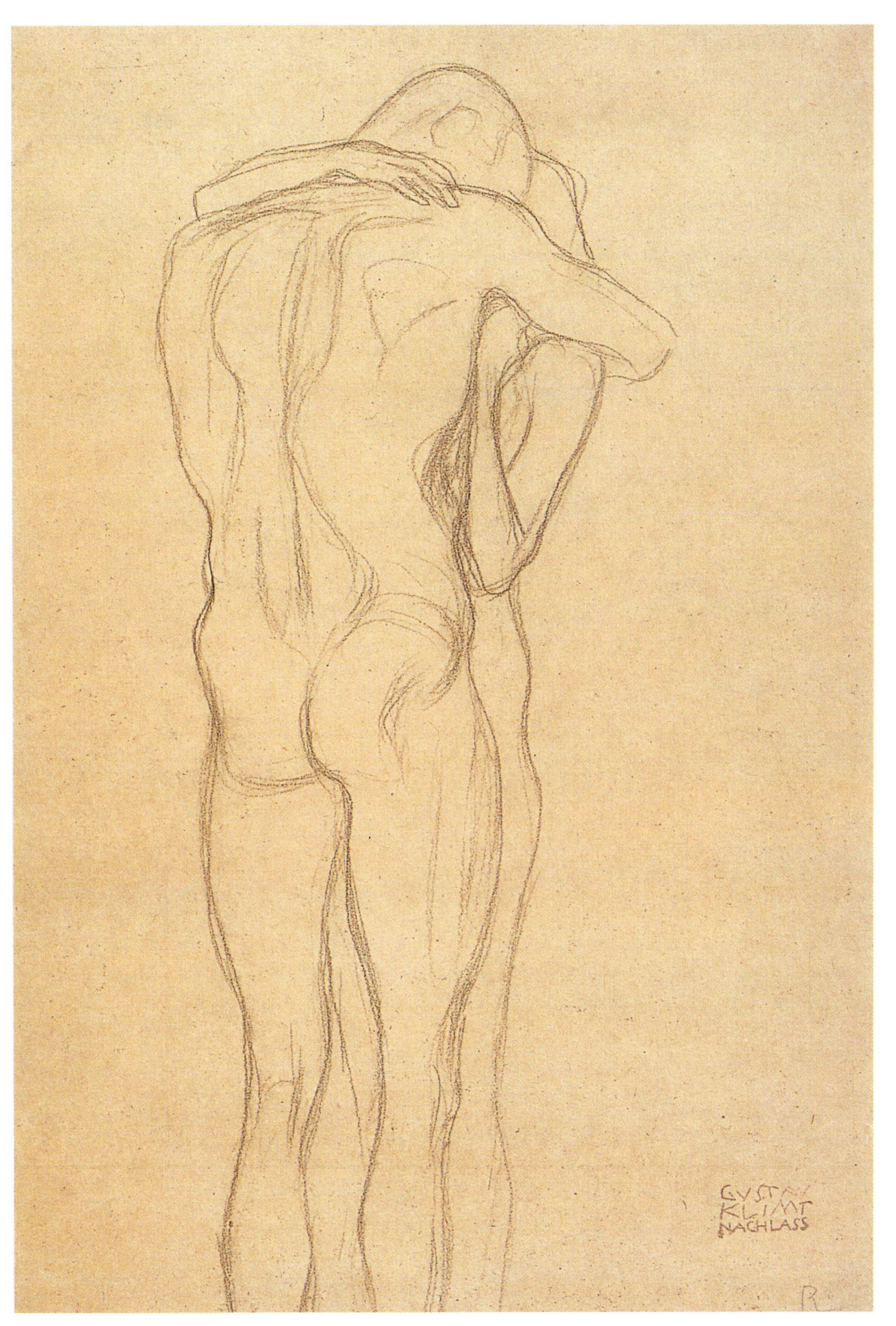

32. ***Two Lovers.***
Sketch for *The Beethoven Frieze,*
Drawing, 45x30.8 cm, Vienna.

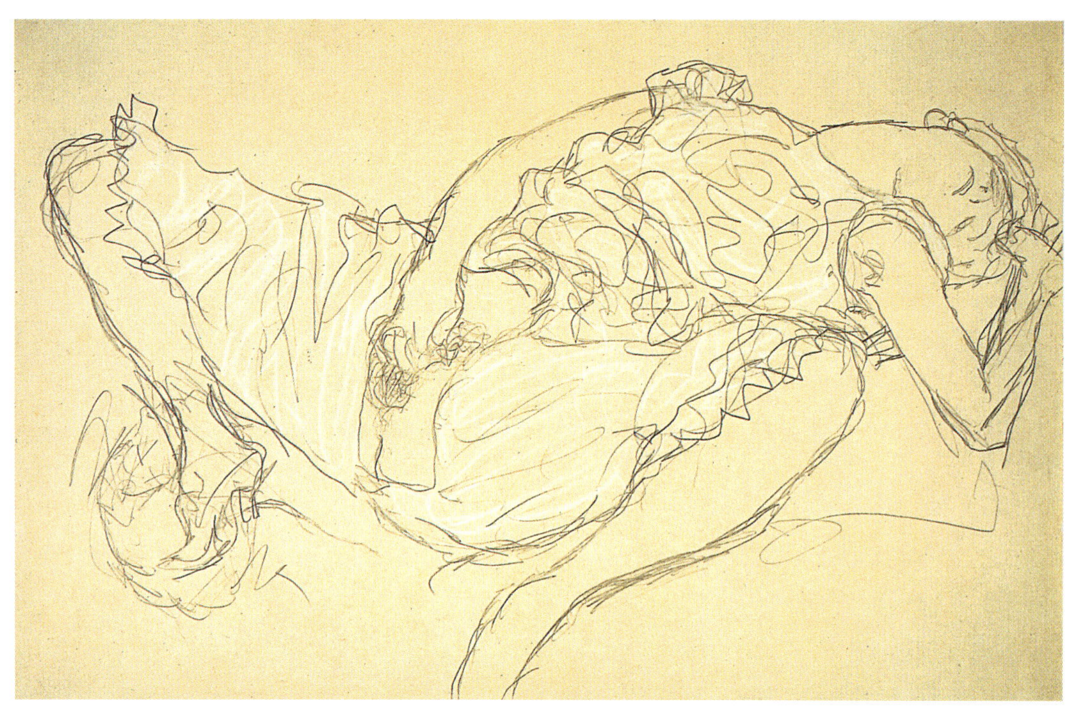

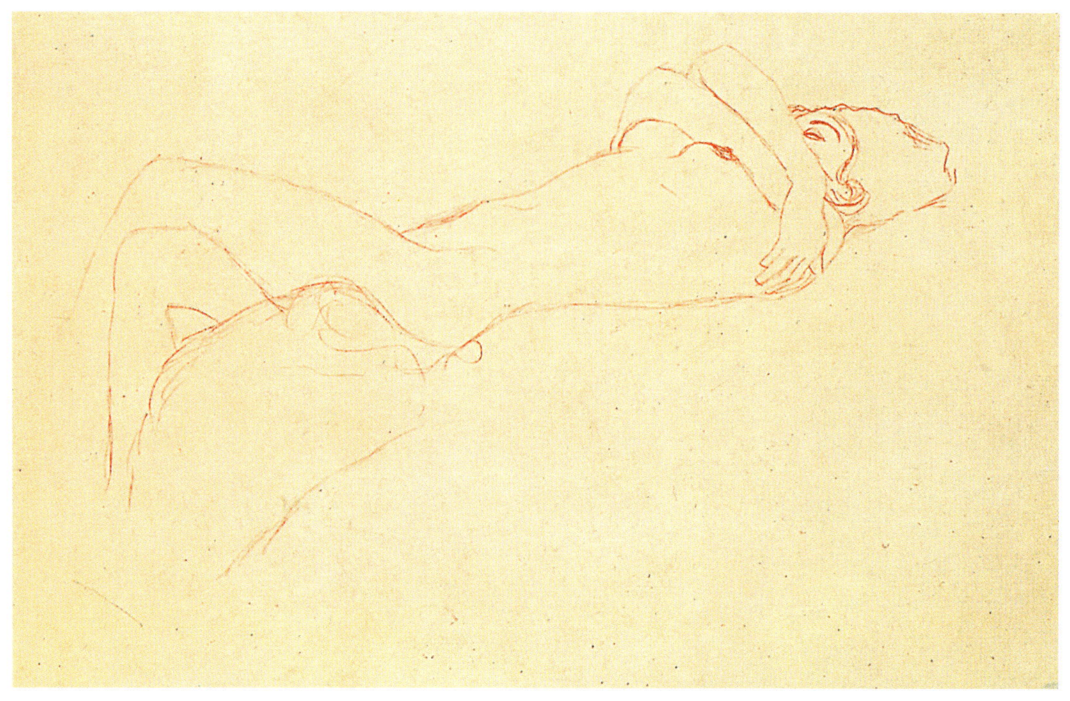

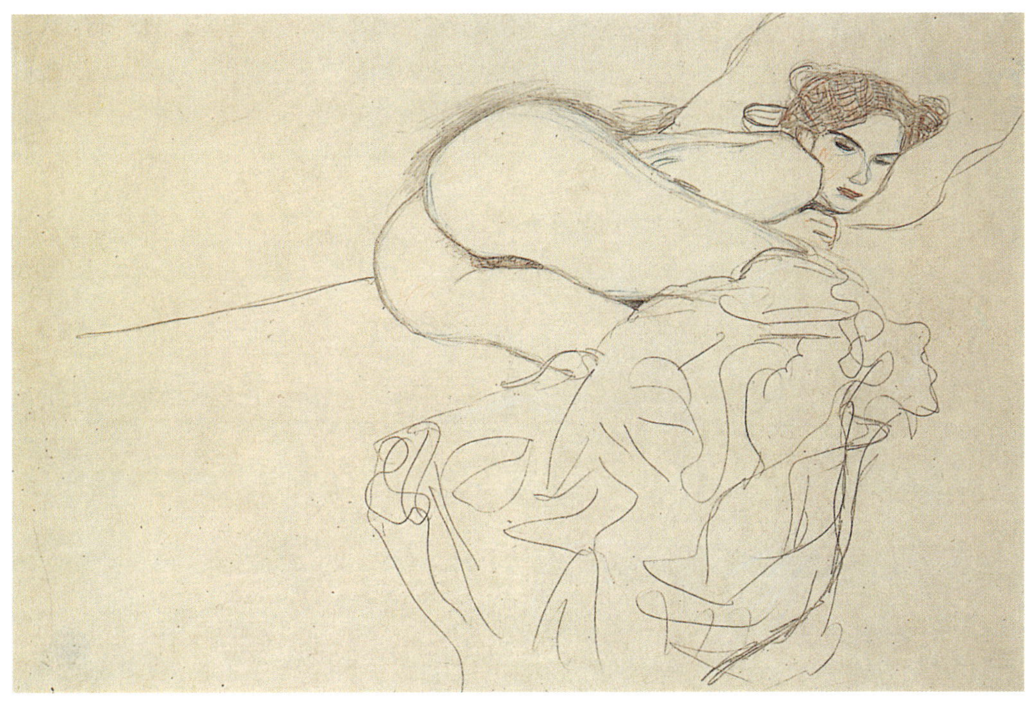

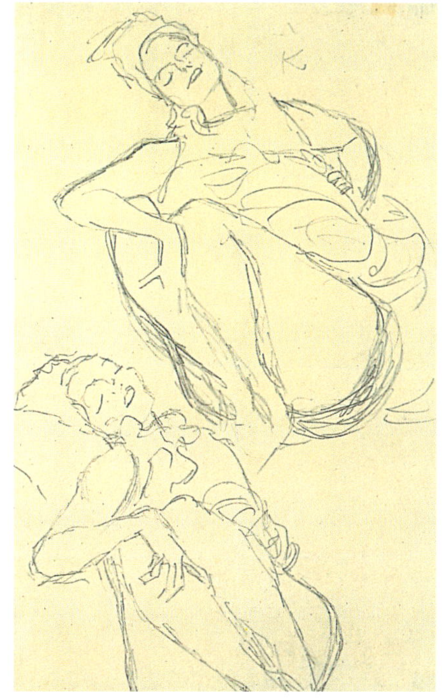

From around 1897 onwards, he spent almost every summer on the Attersee with the Flöge family, periods of peace and tranquillity, which produced the landscape paintings constituting almost a quarter of his entire oeuvre.

The exact nature of Klimt's relationship with Emilie Flöge remains unknown. They never lived together, and although it was Emilie whom Klimt requested on his death bed, there has always been a great deal of speculation as to whether they were actually lovers.

Klimt corresponded extensively both with Emilie and with Marie (Mizzi) Zimmerman, who was the mother of two of his three illegitimate children.

To Marie he writes with great affection and in detail about his work and daily life, whilst to Emilie he appears to write merely in order to communicate information concerning travel arrangements and other such neutral details.

But who is to tell where the truth ultimately lies? It is perfectly possible that more personal correspondence between Klimt and Emilie did exist, but was subsequently destroyed.

33. ***Female Nude wearing lingerie***, 1916-1917.

34. ***Female Nude lying down (in an embracing gesture)***, 1913.

35. ***Nude lying down and huddling***, 1912-1913.

36. ***Two Female Nudes lying down***, 1914-1915.

His 1902 portrait of Emilie shows an attractive young woman wearing one of her own dresses, many of which Klimt designed for her fashion house, as well as jewellery and textiles.

It's a remarkably subdued painting, with just a subtle, tantalising hint of sensuality in the light patch of skin just above the bodice, suggesting the hidden breast beneath.

How different from the 1903 painting *Hope I*, which depicts a naked and heavily pregnant woman, Herma, one of Klimt's favourite models.

The story goes that one day Herma, whom Klimt apparently described as having a backside more beautiful and more intelligent than the faces of many other models, failed to turn up for work.

Klimt, who took very good care of his models, began to worry and finally sent someone to find out if she was ill. Upon hearing that she was not ill but pregnant, Klimt insisted that she came to work anyway. She then became the model for *Hope I* (p. 32).

This fragile, slender woman looking calmly out at the viewer is anything but maternal. Her figure, apart from her distended stomach, is still that of a young woman, thin to the point of skinniness.

Her hair is crowned with flowers as if she were a bride. Depending on one's point of view, her direct gaze and unobscured nakedness shown in profile for maximum effect, are either pointing out the obvious consequences of sex, or inviting a still-sexual response to her body.

The later *Hope II* (p. 33), painted in 1907-8, has a far more maternal feel. The woman's breasts are full and large-nippled, her head bowed in a peaceful, almost madonna-like pose.

She is enclosed by a fabric that follows an abruptly straight line down her back as if she were actually sitting on a straight-backed chair and was being carried by the figures underneath her. The last great hope of humankind, transported on the backs of other women.

37. ***Girlfriends***, 1905.
Black chalk,
45 x 31 cm, Vienna,
Historisches Museum.

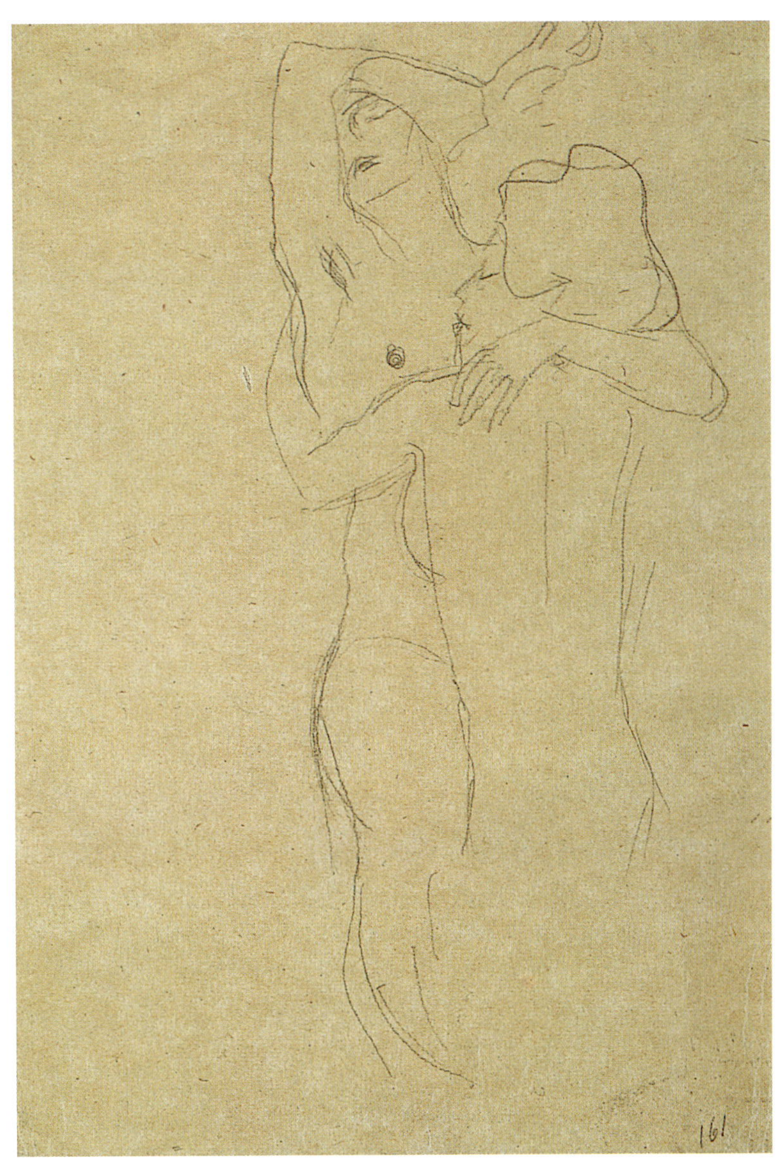

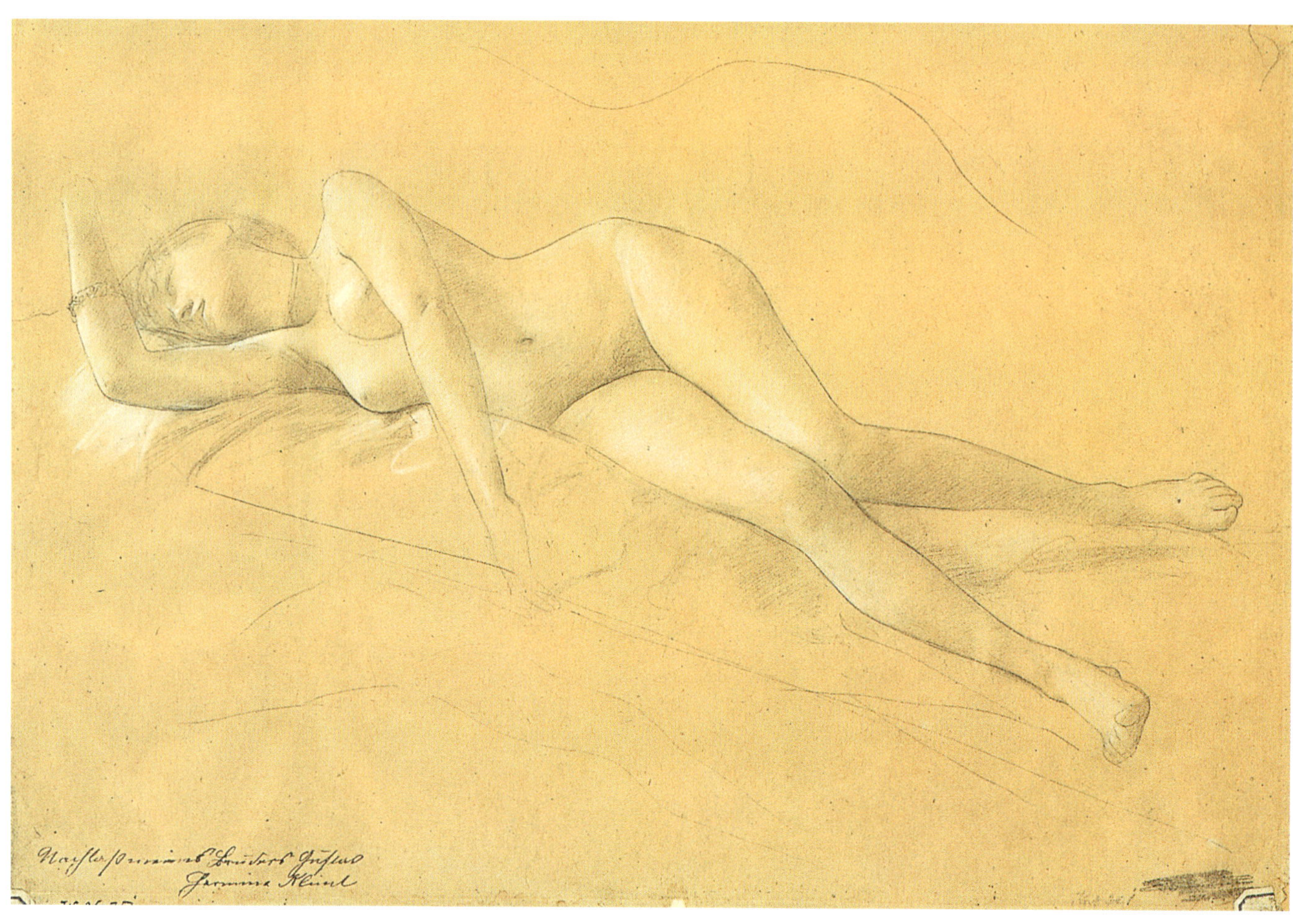

38. ***Female Nude lying Down***.

39. ***Woman Seated with Open Thighs***, 1916.
Graphite, white highlights, red pencil, 57 x 38 cm,
Private Collection.

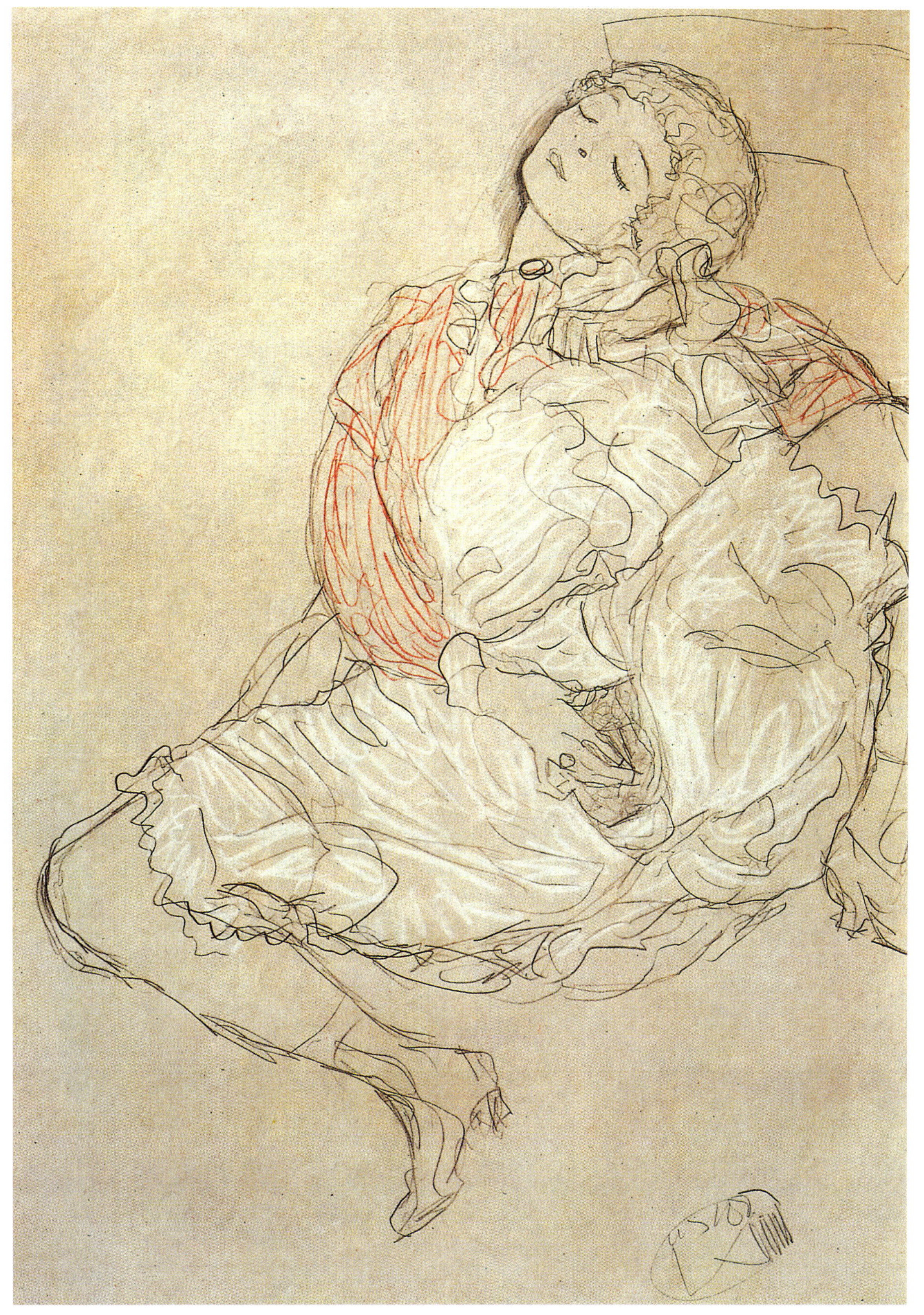

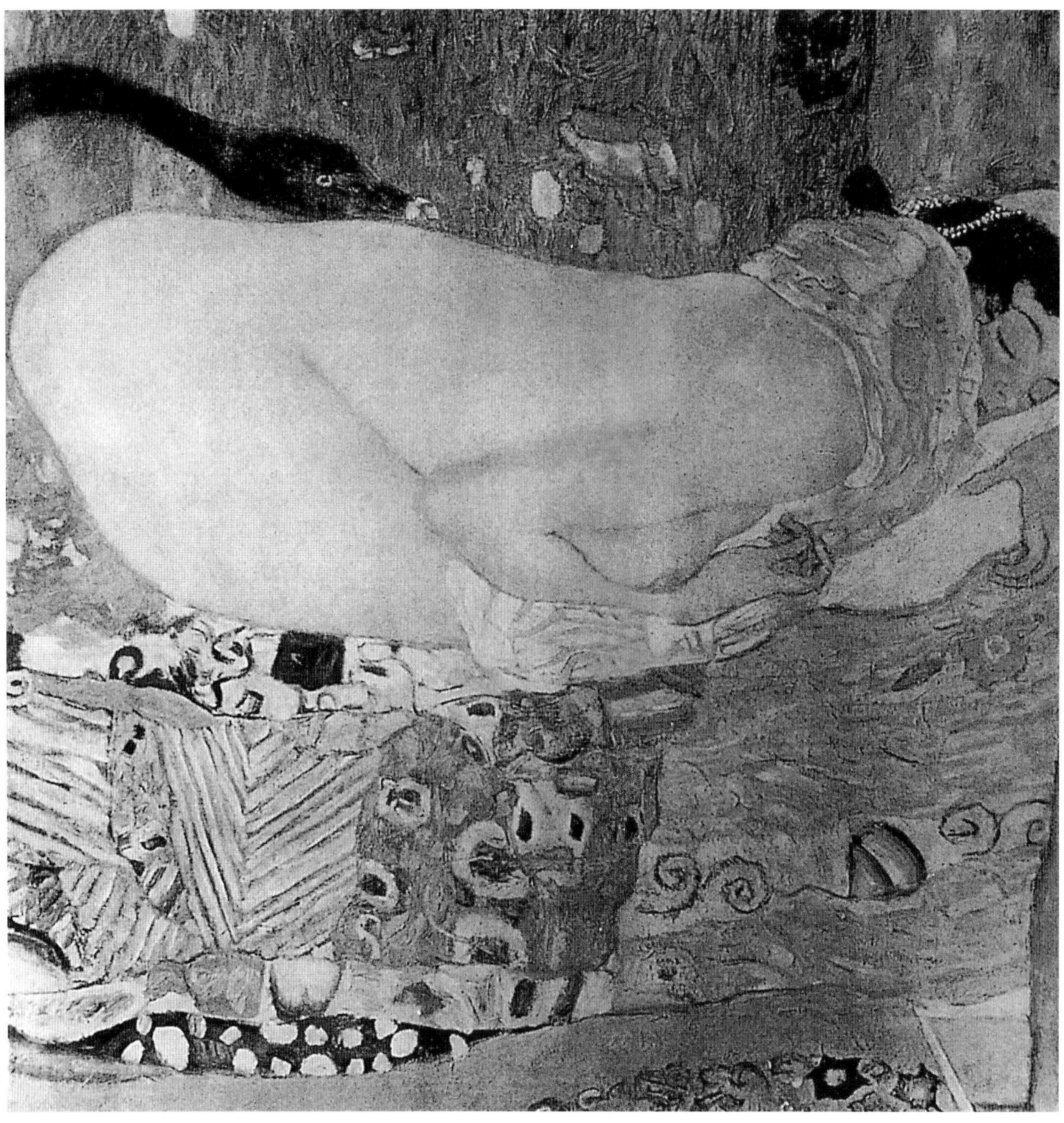

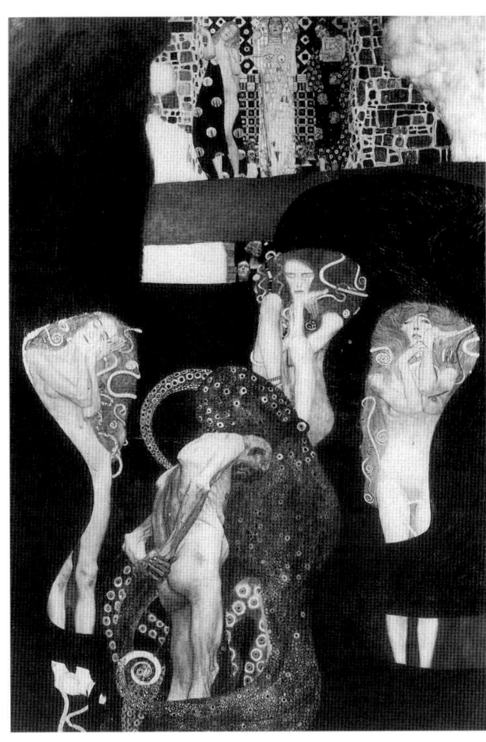

When Klimt died, there were no fewer than fourteen claims that he was the father of an illegitimate child, only three of which were legally upheld - two by Marie Zimmerman and one by Maria Ucicky. (The child was named Gustav after his father and later went on to become a film director).

It is generally assumed that he slept with most of his models. He was certainly known to be very generous towards them. Who knows whether the pregnancies depicted in his paintings had any connection with the painter himself? If they did, Herma's gaze in *Hope I* takes on an entirely new meaning: a look of reproach? Or one of irony?

Drawings and sketches

In his studio, Klimt kept girls available to him at all times, waiting for him in a room next door in case he decided to paint them. Franz Servaes, a contemporary art critic, observed: "Here he was surrounded by mysterious, naked female creatures, who, while he stood silent in front of his easel, strolled around his studio, stretching themselves, lazing around and enjoying the day - always ready for the command of

40. ***Leda.***

41. ***Jurisprudence***, 1907. Oil on canvas, 430 x 300 cm, burned in 1945.

the master obediently to stand still whenever he caught sight of a pose or a movement that appealed to his sense of beauty and that he would then capture in a rapid drawing."

Klimt made sketches for virtually everything he did. Sometimes there were over a hundred drawings for one painting, each showing a different detail - a piece of clothing or jewellery, or a simple gesture.

They would lie about his studio in heaps, where his adored cats, it is said, had a habit of destroying them.

Unfortunately, the bulk of his sketchbooks were destroyed not by cats but by a fire in Emilie Flöge's apartment. Only three of the books survived.

The drawings which have survived, however, provide a fascinating insight into Klimt's artistic and personal preoccupations: whereas in his paintings nudity and sexuality are covered, almost imprisoned by ornament and textile to be partially and tantalisingly revealed, in his drawings eroticism is open and undisguised.

Even during his lifetime, his drawings were by some critics regarded as the best work of his entire oevre, but they would not have been widely seen.

Unlike Schiele, who earned his living from his drawings, Klimt's income was derived entirely from his painting.

Drawing for him was either a necessary preparatory process or a form of relaxation, a way of expressing himself spontaneously free from the constraints and detail of oil.

Klimt's drawings not only reveal his mastery of draughtsmanship, they also show an erotic obsession and a sexual freedom quite at odds with the covered-up, repressed society in which he moved.

In these drawings there is no visual, temporal, or spacial context, just the women themselves, who were presumably, as earlier described, wandering around his studio in a state of undress.

42. ***The Kiss***, 1907-1908. Oil on canvas, 180 x 180 cm, Vienna, Österreichische Galerie.

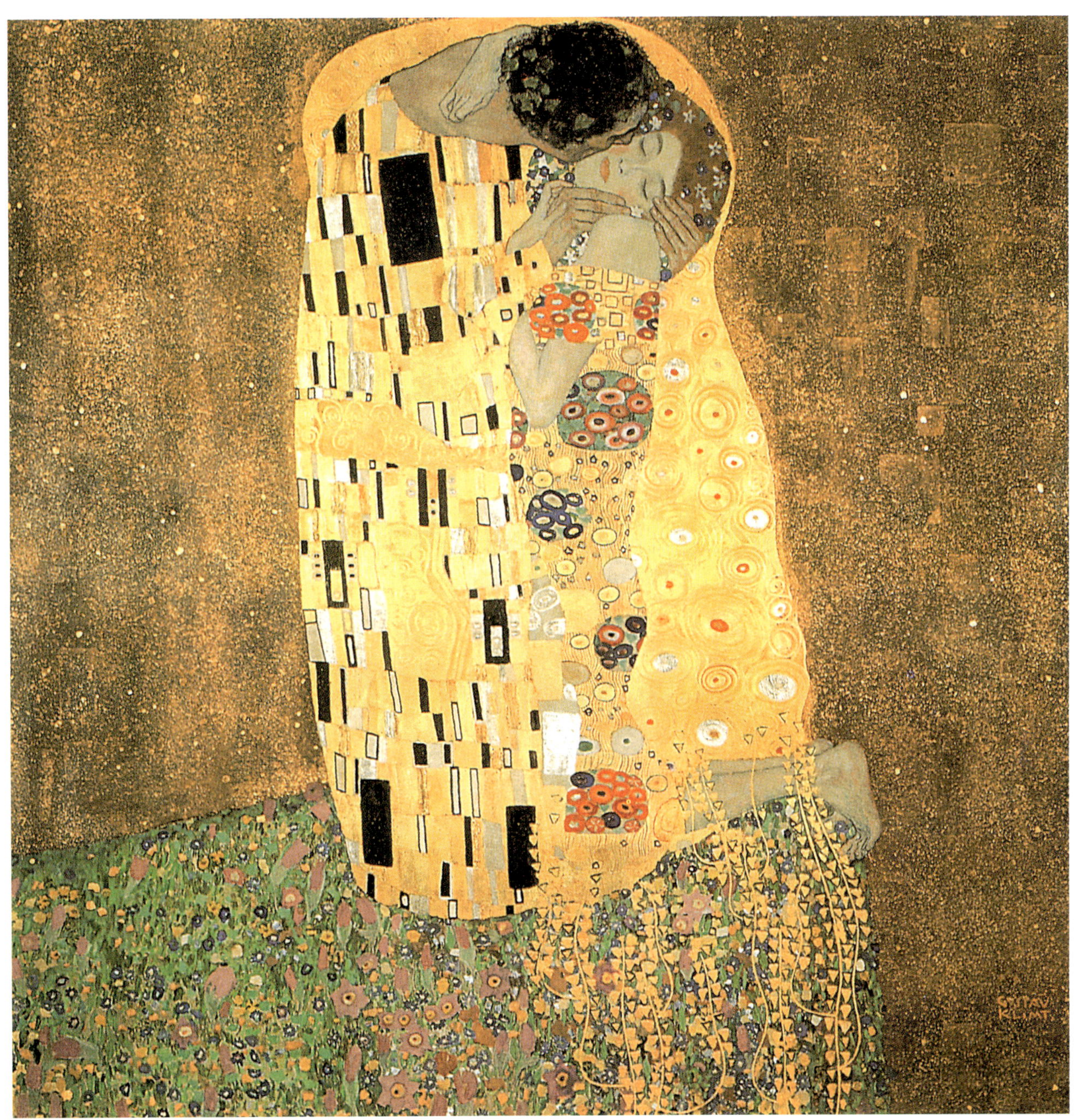

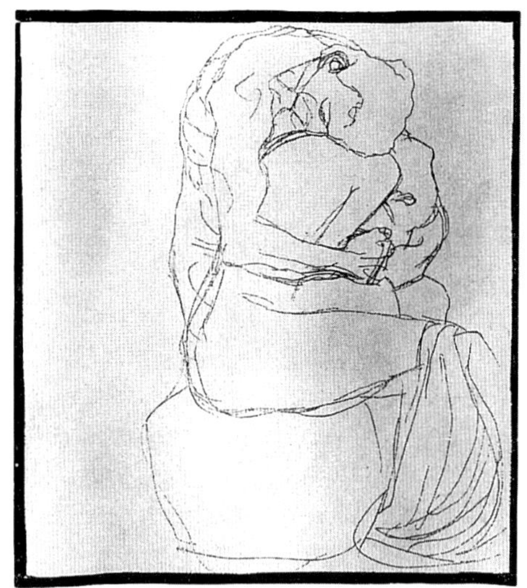
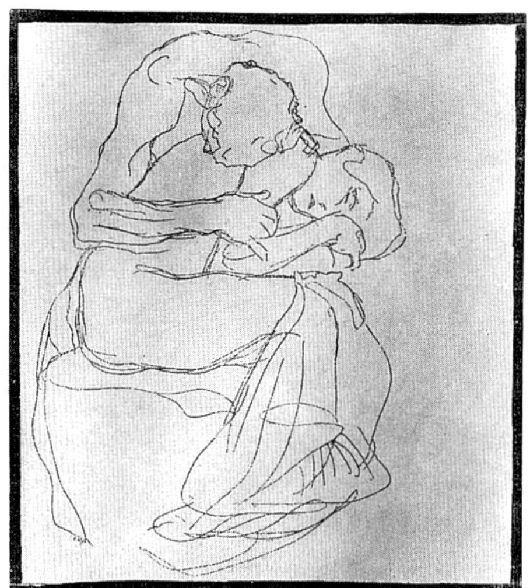
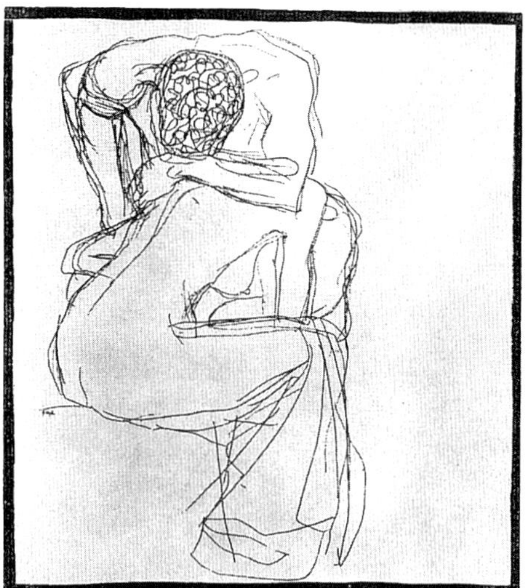

He draws them only in outline, omitting any internal modelling or shading of their bodies and almost always drawing attention to their genitalia or breasts by using perspective, foreshortening, distortion or other formal techniques.

A wonderful example of how a couple of pencil strokes can be used to devastatingly erotic effect is the 1905-6 drawing *Friends Embracing* (p. 34), in which a tiny circle of darkness draws the viewer's gaze automatically between the woman's legs and her buttocks.

The women are frequently depicted masturbating, absorbed in their own sensual pleasures, eyes closed, face slightly averted.

How very at ease these women must have felt with Klimt to allow him to portray them in this way! Langorous, feline, and utterly absorbed, they masturbate delicately, fingers poised above the clitoris, still fully or partially clothed, eyes closed in the imaginary heat of a summer's afternoon.

Sometimes Klimt draws in great detail, sometimes it is the overall pose that clearly interests him. Men rarely make an appearance in these drawings, and when they do they are almost uniquely depicted with their back to the viewer.

43. ***Lovers, Studies***, 1903. Black chalk.

44. ***The Kiss (Detail)***, 1907-1908. Oil on canvas, 180 x 180 cm, Vienna, Österreichische Galerie.

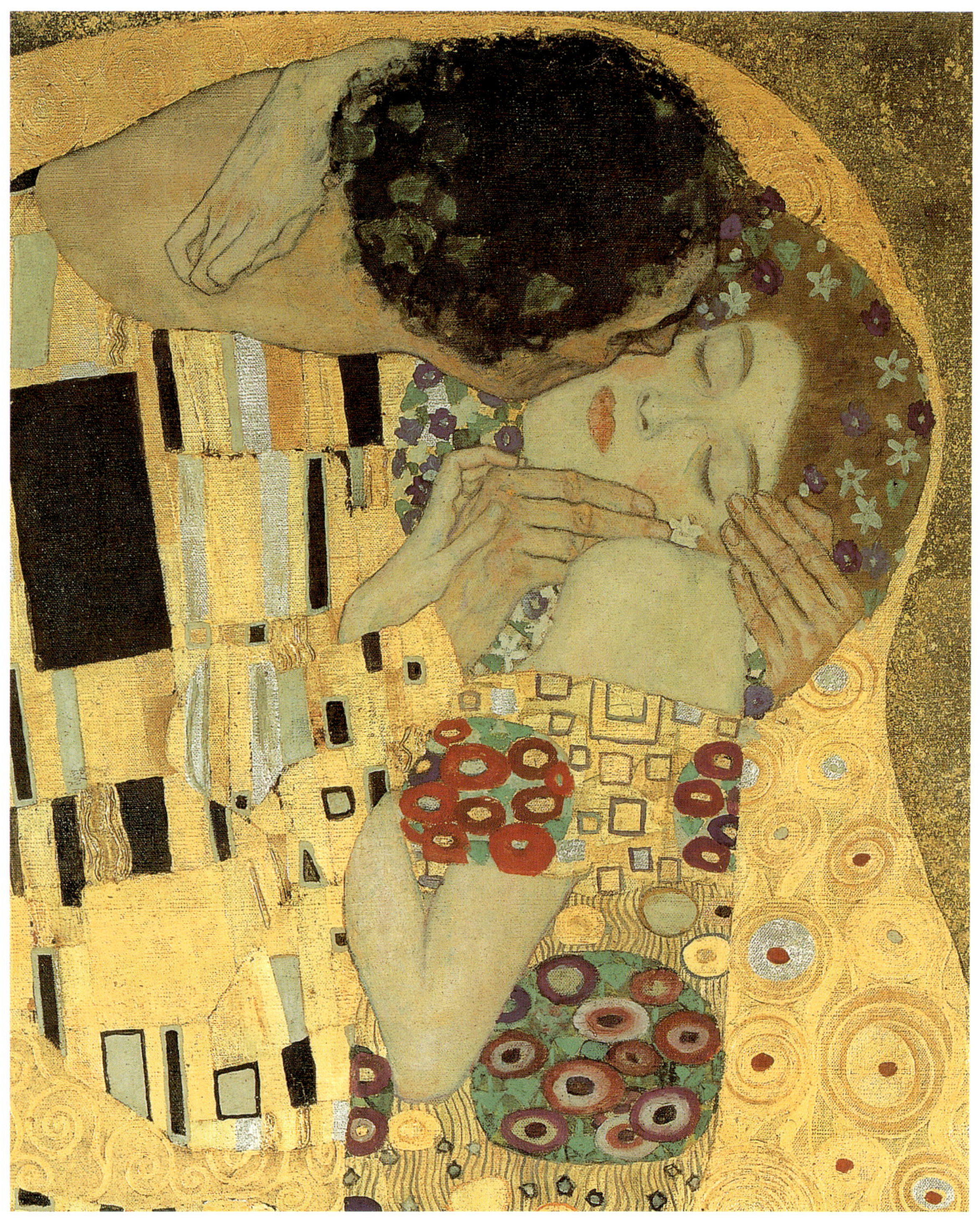

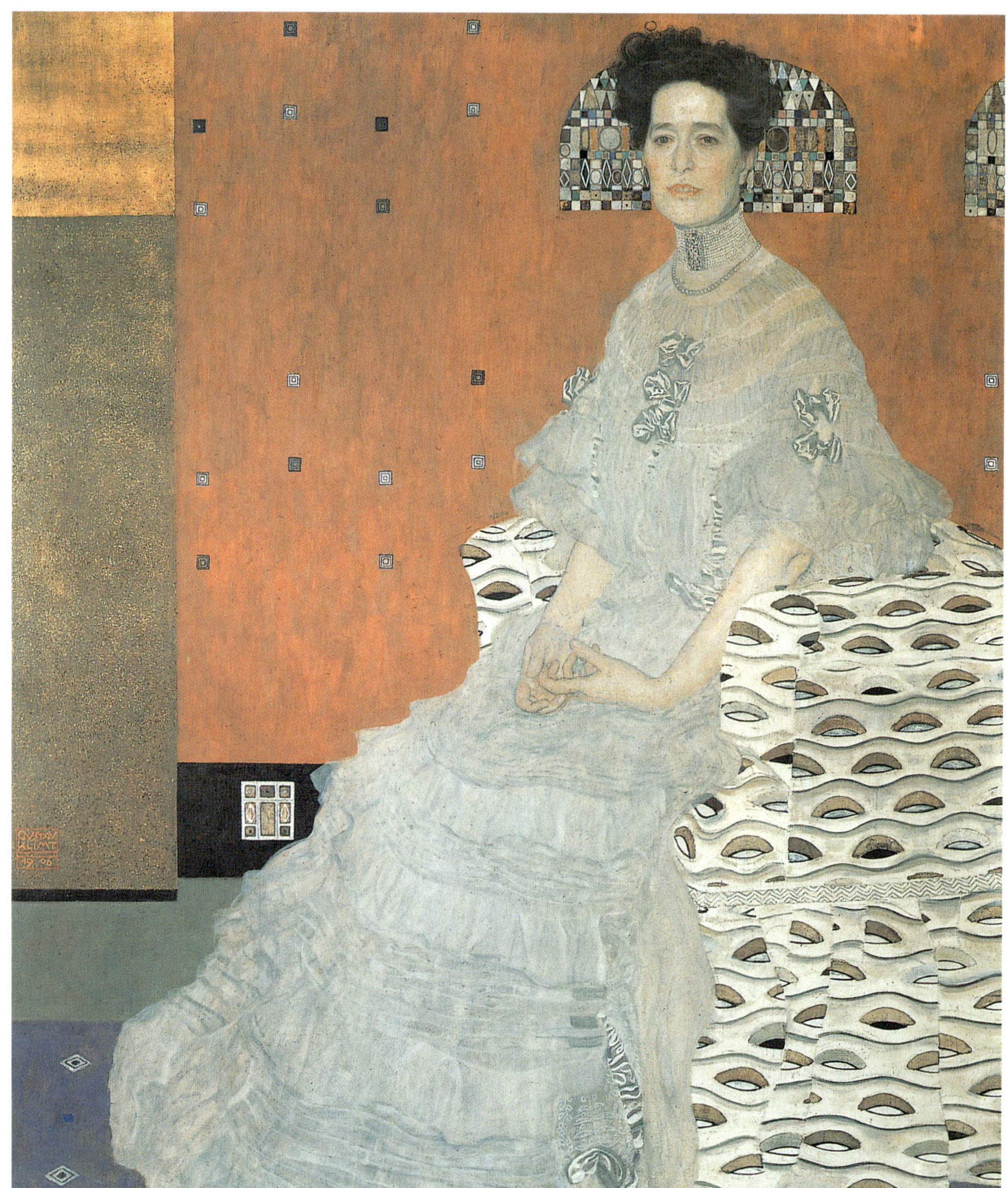

45. ***Portrait of Fritza Riedler.***
1906,
Österreichische Galerie,
Vienna.

46. ***Portrait of Adele Bloch-Bauer I.***
1907,
Österreichische Galerie,
Vienna.

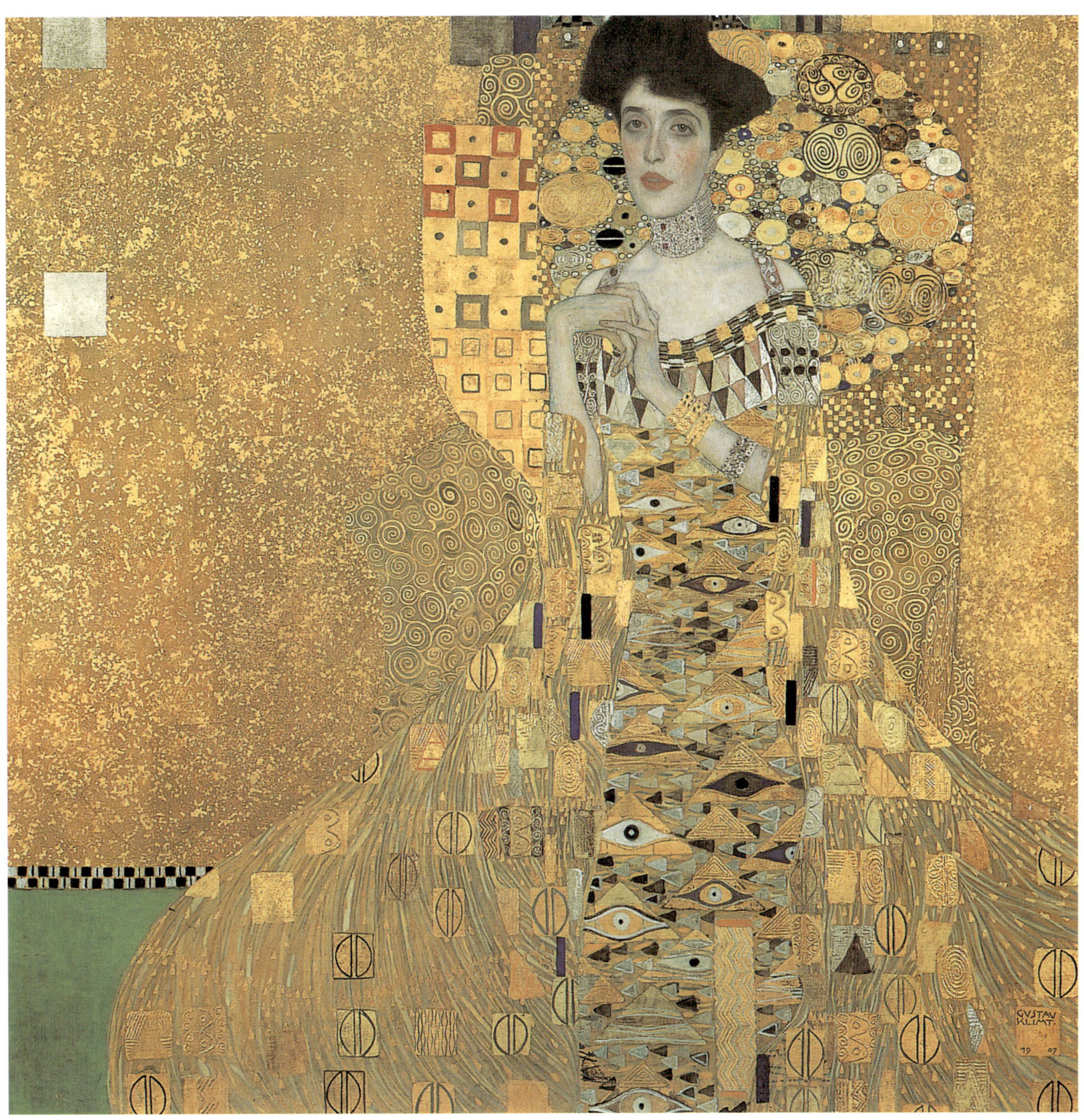
GVSTAV
KLIMT.
19 07

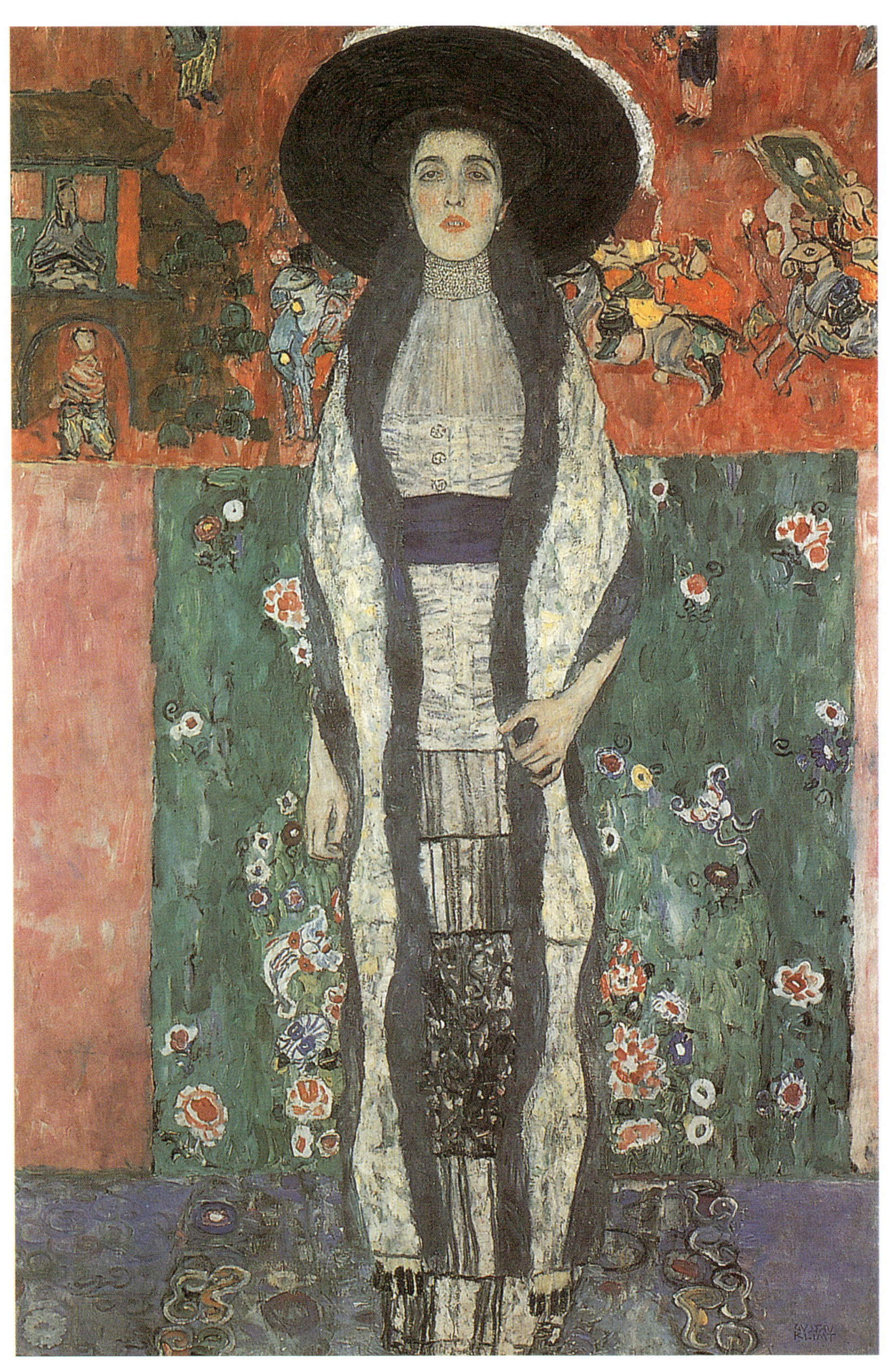

47. ***Portrait of Adele Bloch-Bauer II.***

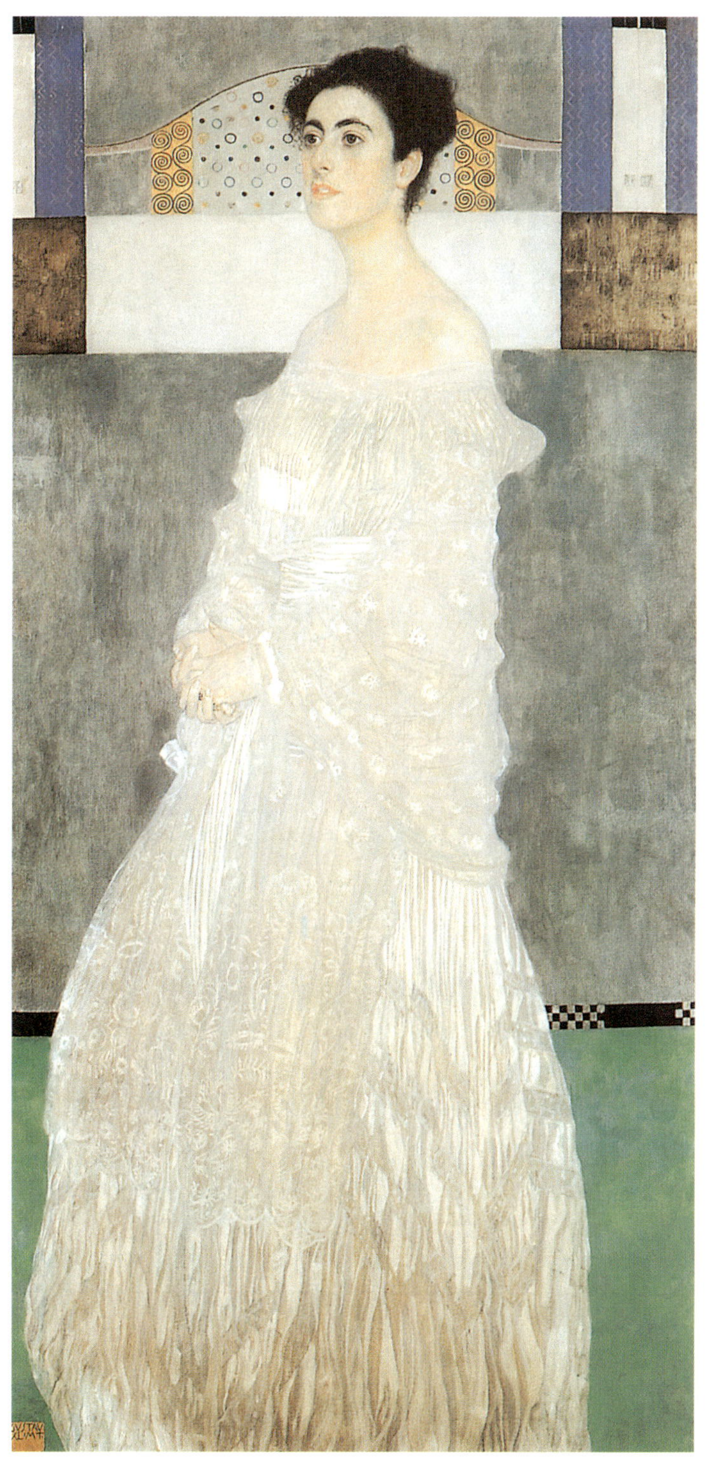

48. ***Portrait of Margaret Stonborough-Wittgenstein.***

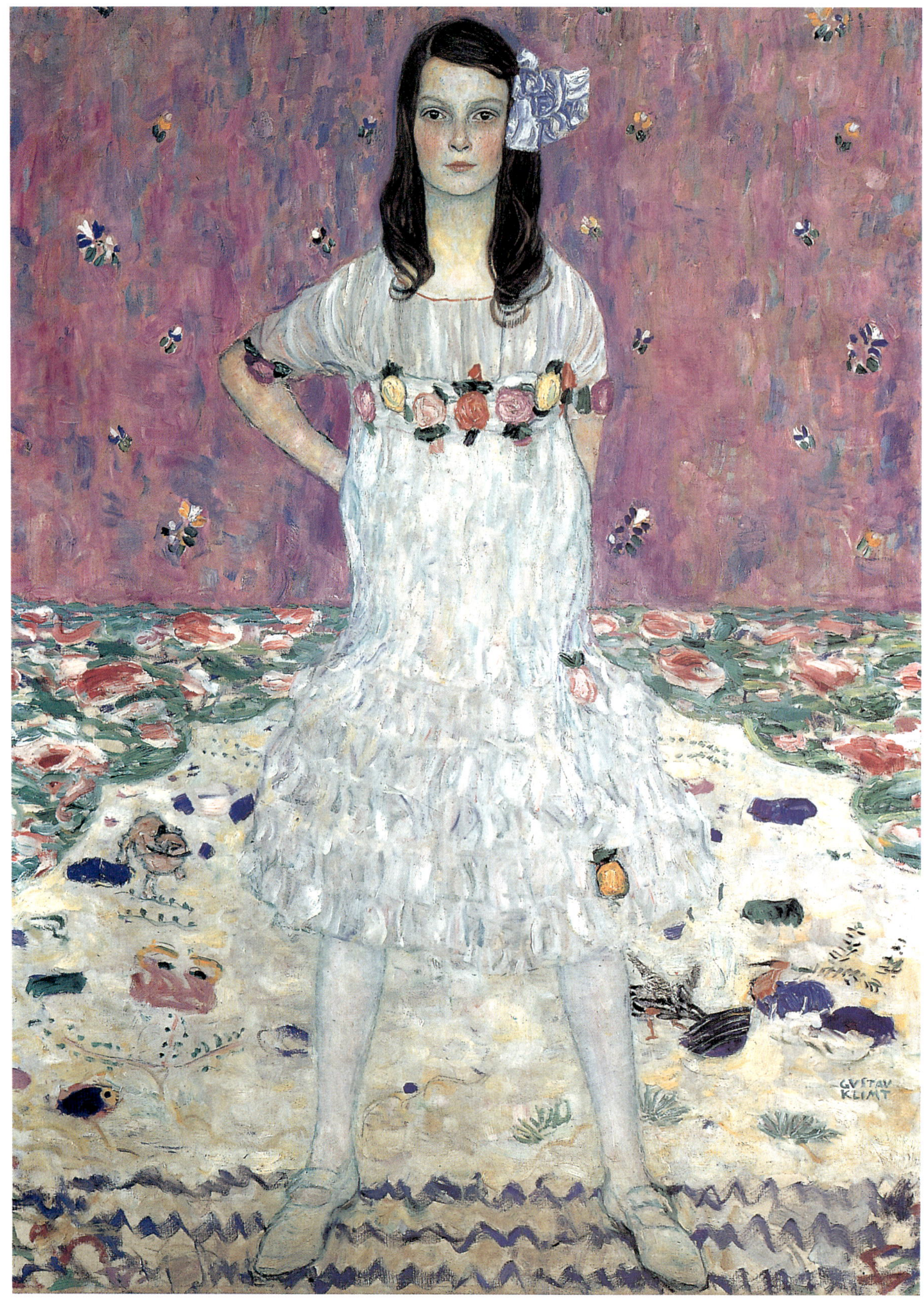
GVSTAV
KLIMT

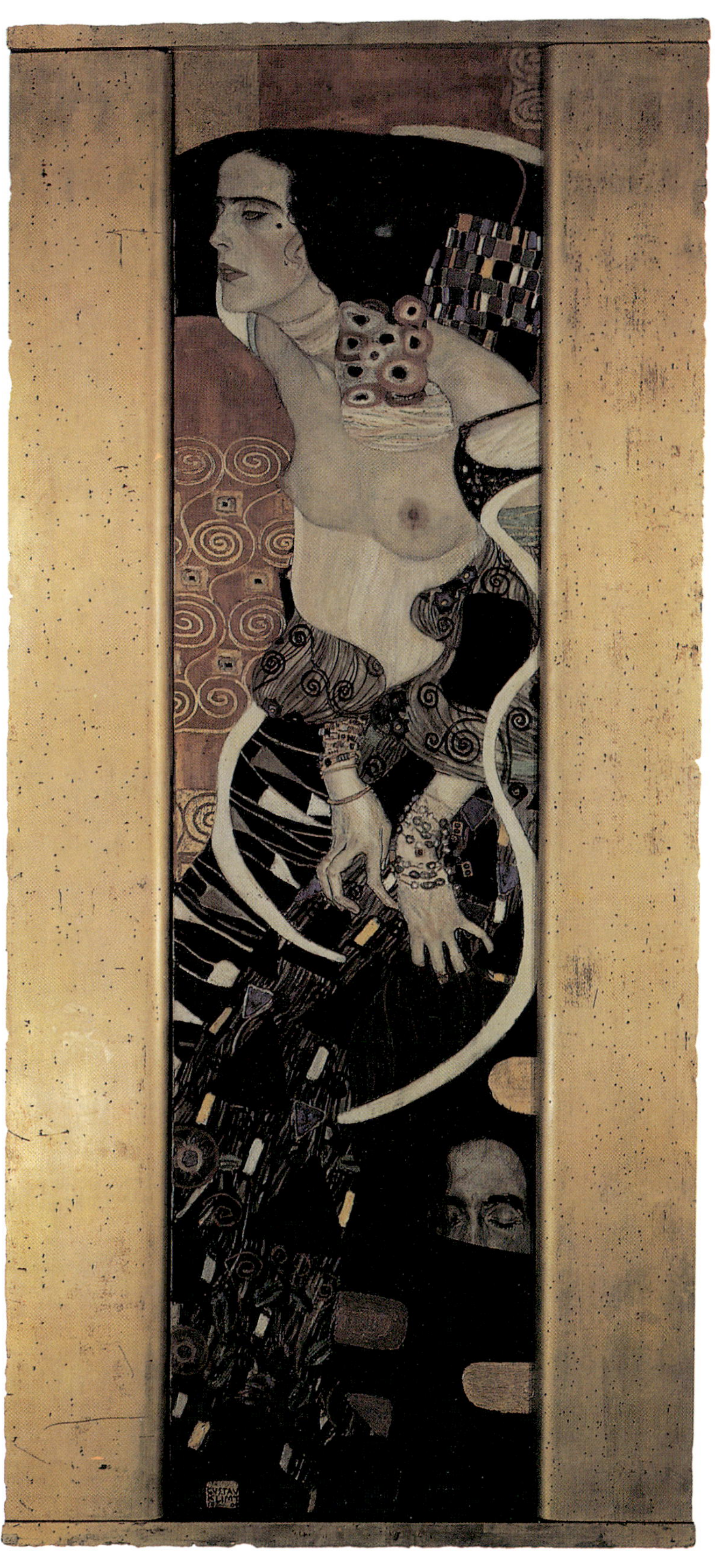

49. ***Portrait of Mäda Primavesi.*** 1913, Oil on canvas, 149.9x 110.5 cm, The Metropolitan Museum of Art, New York.

50. ***Judith II***, 1909. Oil on canvas, 178 x 46 cm, Venice.

In general, apart from academic studies at art school, men are peripheral figures in Klimt's paintings.

Their faces are rarely shown, and they seem to exist either as voyeurs or simply as the physical partner to a sexual act, of which the woman is the main point of interest for the viewer.

What is extraordinary in Klimt's work is that, while expressing his clear admiration for women's beauty, when he shows men and women together he articulates a kind of remoteness, a gulf between the sexes.

In his painting *The Kiss* (p. 45, 47), the man's face cannot be seen. He holds the woman up, his hands clasped round her face in a gesture of great tenderness, yet her face is turned away from his embrace: he is offered only her cheek to kiss, and her hand looks almost as if she were trying to pull his away.

Auguste Rodin's earlier sculpture *The Kiss*, by contrast, shows both lovers fully engaged in their embrace.

It is a tender, romantic and sensual moment equally involving both partners. One could assuredly interpret this lack of direct contact in Klimt's painting in other terms - her face is turned towards us so that we can admire its peaceful beauty, for example - but another sketch of 1903-4 presents a series of images that underline the first interpretation: the figures are seated in a pose similar to that of the lovers in Rodin's sculpture.

The man, however, seems unable to make any physical contact with the woman, desperately though he tries. He clasps her to him, leans over her, and finally leans on top of her in an attitude of despair.

Are we to infer from this a vision of the world in which men desperately seek love from women who, though appearing open to this contact, actually possess a quiet, independent world quite inaccessible to men?

51. ***Bride (Unfinished)***, 1917-1918. Oil on canvas, 166 x 190 cm, Private Collection.

One of Klimt's amorous liaisons might suggest so. Alma Mahler-Werfel (then Schindler) knew Klimt when she was a young girl of seventeen and claims that he was in love with her.

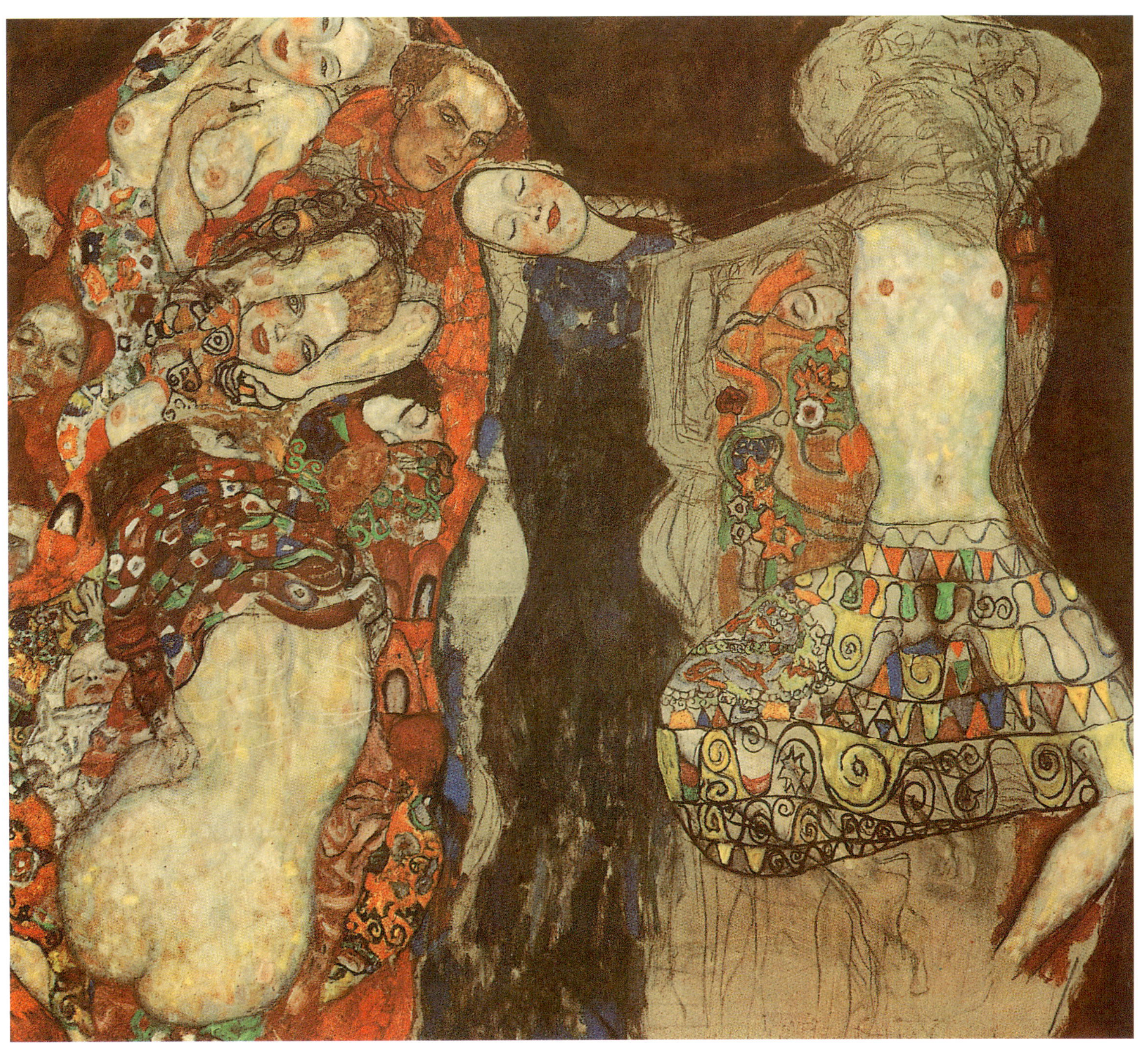

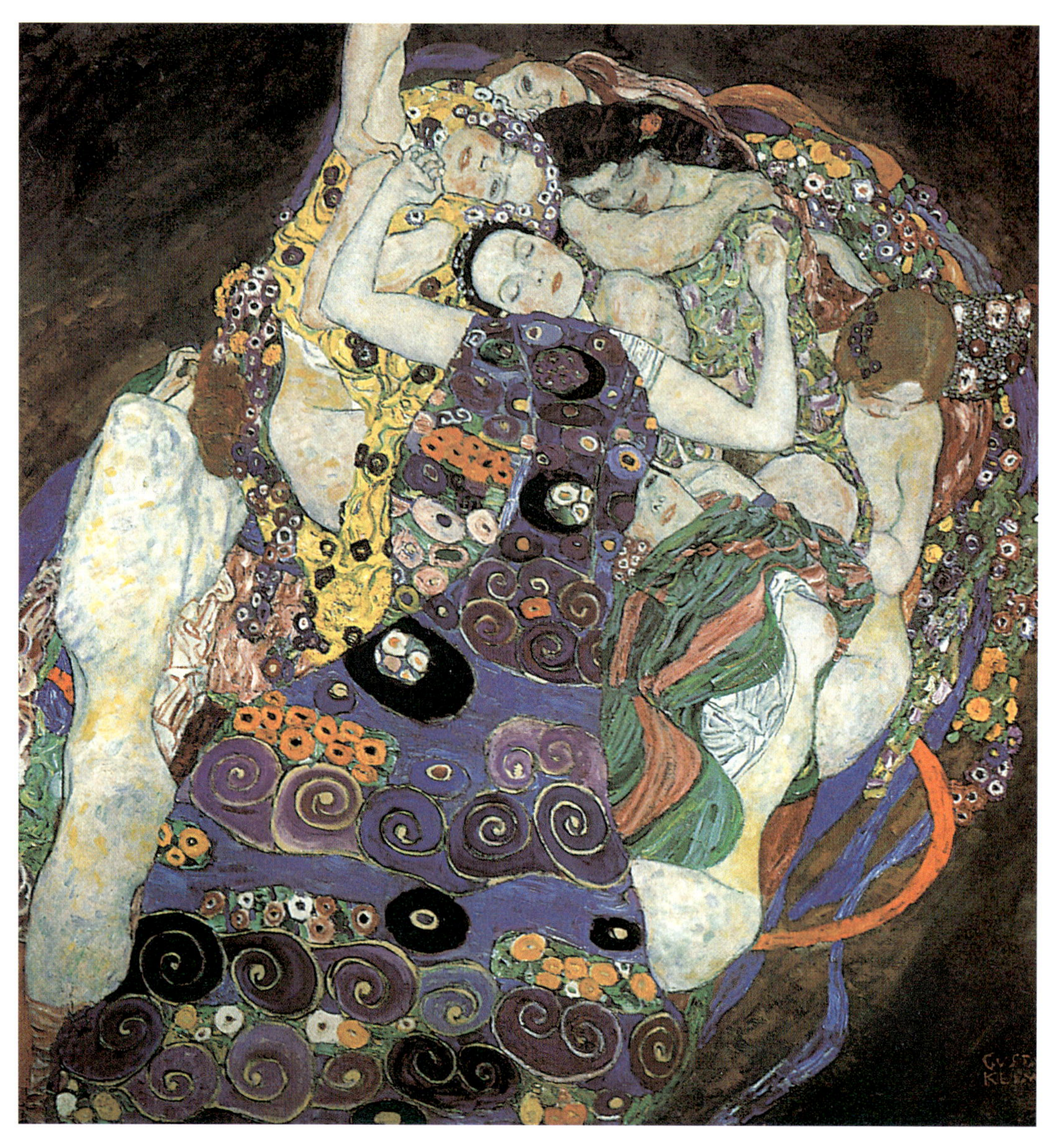

52. ***Virgin***, 1913. Oil on canvas, 190 x 200 cm, Prague.

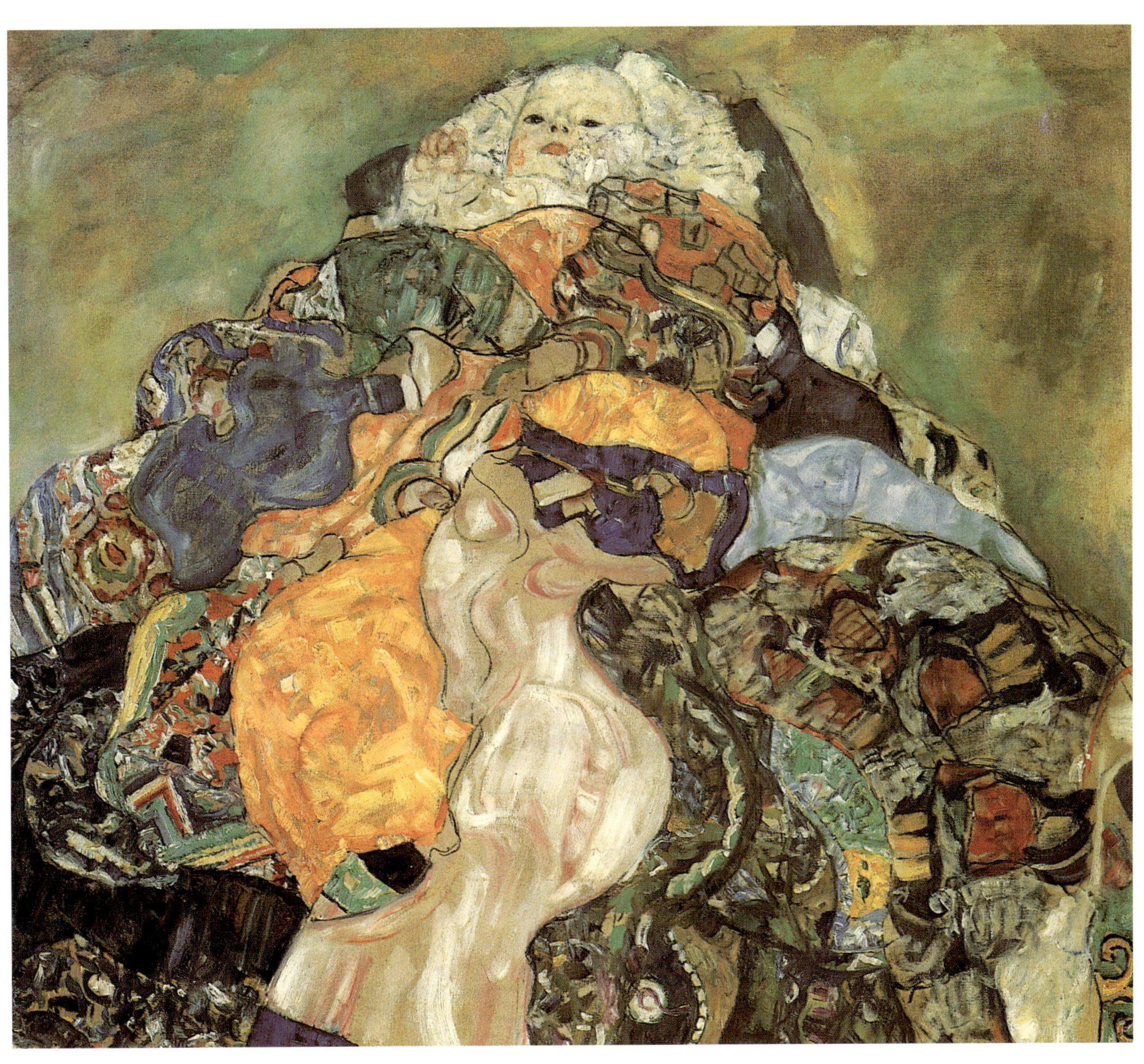

53. ***Baby (Detail)***, 1917-1918. Oil on canvas, 110 x 110 cm, Washington, National Gallery.

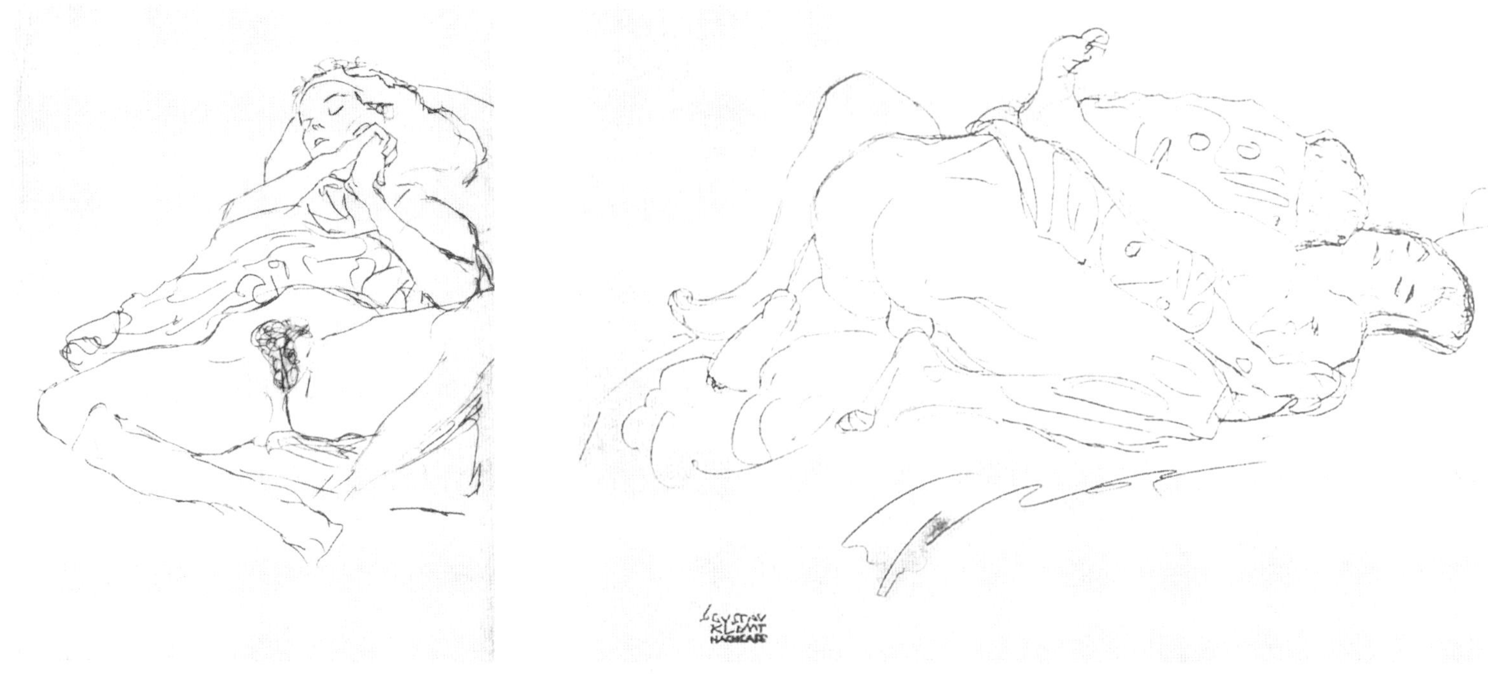

She is not a modest diarist by any means, but there is no reason to doubt the truth of the affair, especially in the light of a later letter of apology written by Klimt to her stepfather, Carl Moll.

Alma later made something of a career out of having relationships with artists: she was married three times, first to Gustav Mahler, then to the architect Walter Gropius, then finally to the Prague poet Franz Werfel, with a wild love affair with Oskar Kokoschka thrown in for good measure in between.

Of her youthful infatuation with Klimt she writes: "He was the most gifted of them all, thirty-five years of age, at the zenith of his powers, beautiful in every sense of the word and already famous.

His beauty and my youthful freshness, his genius, my talents, the profound life-melody we shared touched the same chords in us both.

54. ***Semi-nude sitting and leaning.***

55. ***Lovers.***

56. ***Danäe.***

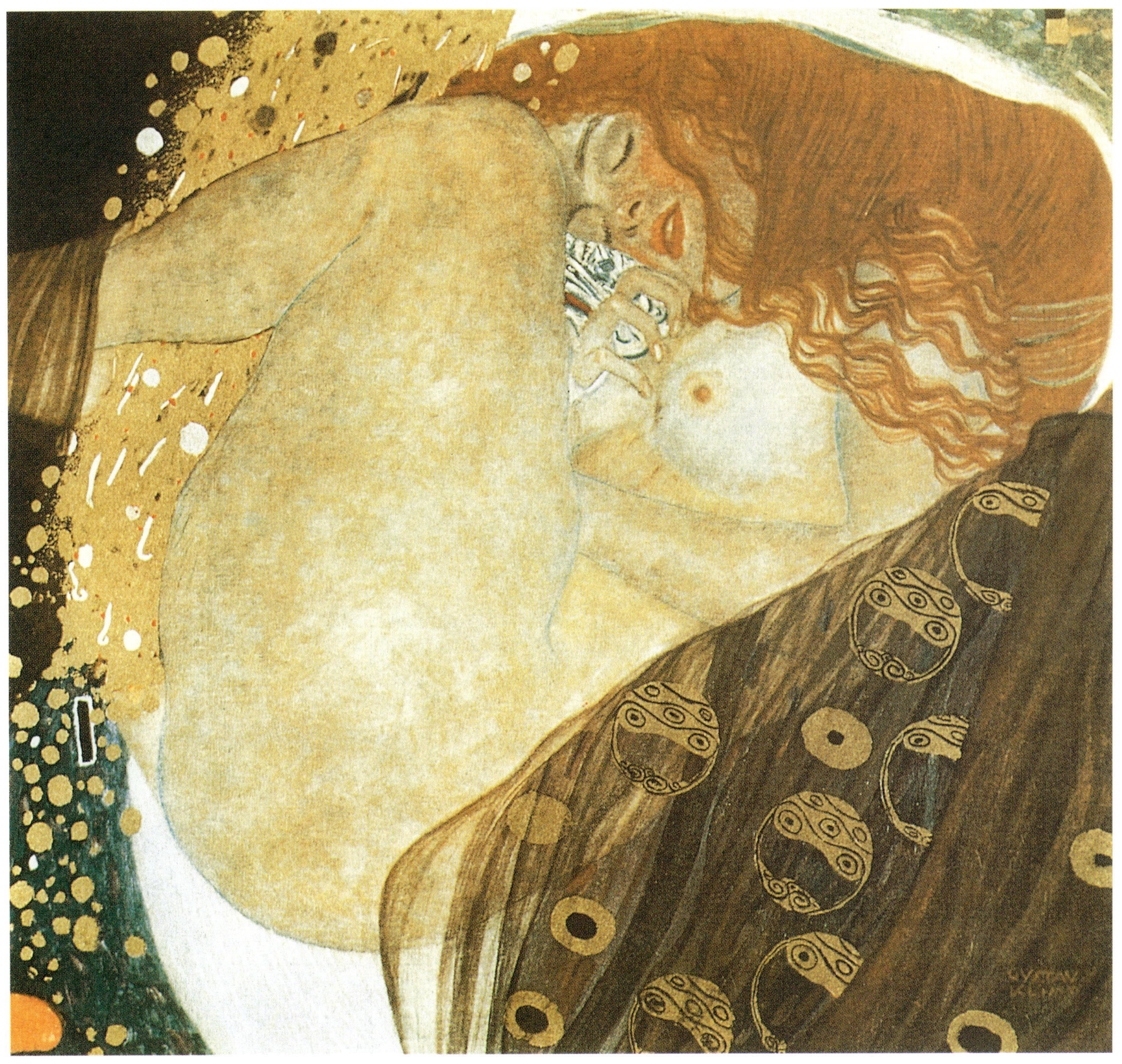

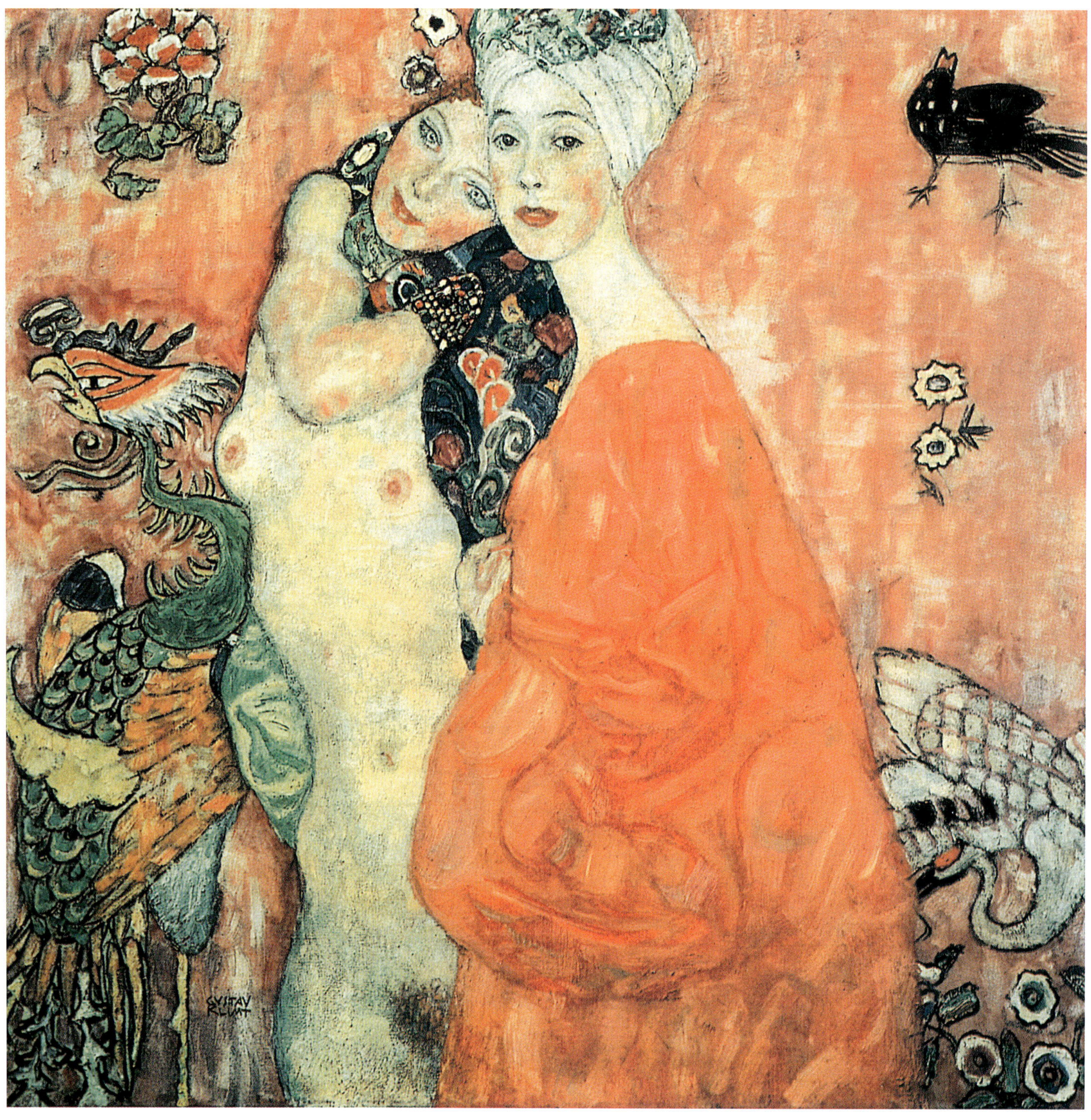
GVSTAV
KLIMT

I was ridiculously ignorant of all things passionate - and he felt and found me everywhere ... He was bound by a hundred chains: women, children, even sisters who fought over him. But he still followed me..."

Society portraits

The freedom of Klimt's drawings stands in marked contrast to the portraits of society women he produced between 1903 and around 1913.

Where the women in his drawings are unconstrained either by clothes or by social conventions, he depicts Fritza Riedler and Adele Bloch-Bauer awash in a sea of pattern and ornament. Their faces stand out, serious and composed, before blocks of pattern or colour strategically placed behind their heads to emphasize their features to the maximum.

Their bodies are submerged in swathes of textile patterns merging with the background so that the face appears isolated, fragile, alone.

The portrait of Margaret Stonborough-Wittgenstein is notable as one of the few which is not dominated by pattern, and is a clear tribute to the work of Whistler, whom Klimt much admired.

There is also something particularly striking in the gaze and stance of the young Maria Primavesi: she stands, hand on hip, legs apart, the age-old combination of innocence and provocation. These are remarkably delicate portraits.

Each face betrays so much about the sitter - a calmness, or an awkwardness, and in Adele Bloch-Bauer's, the only one of these women known also to have been Klimt's lover, it is difficult not to read into her face a desire to pose as luxuriously as Klimt's models did, especially in the 1912 portrait, where her open lips, her gaze, and her direct stance suggest a certain sexual readiness in stark contrast to the upright behaviour which would undoubtedly have been expected of her.

Pattern and nudity

In Klimt's paintings from the last ten years of his life, pattern, textile and ornament are used to highly erotic effect, emphasizing the nakedness of the body rather than covering it.

57. ***Girlfriends.***

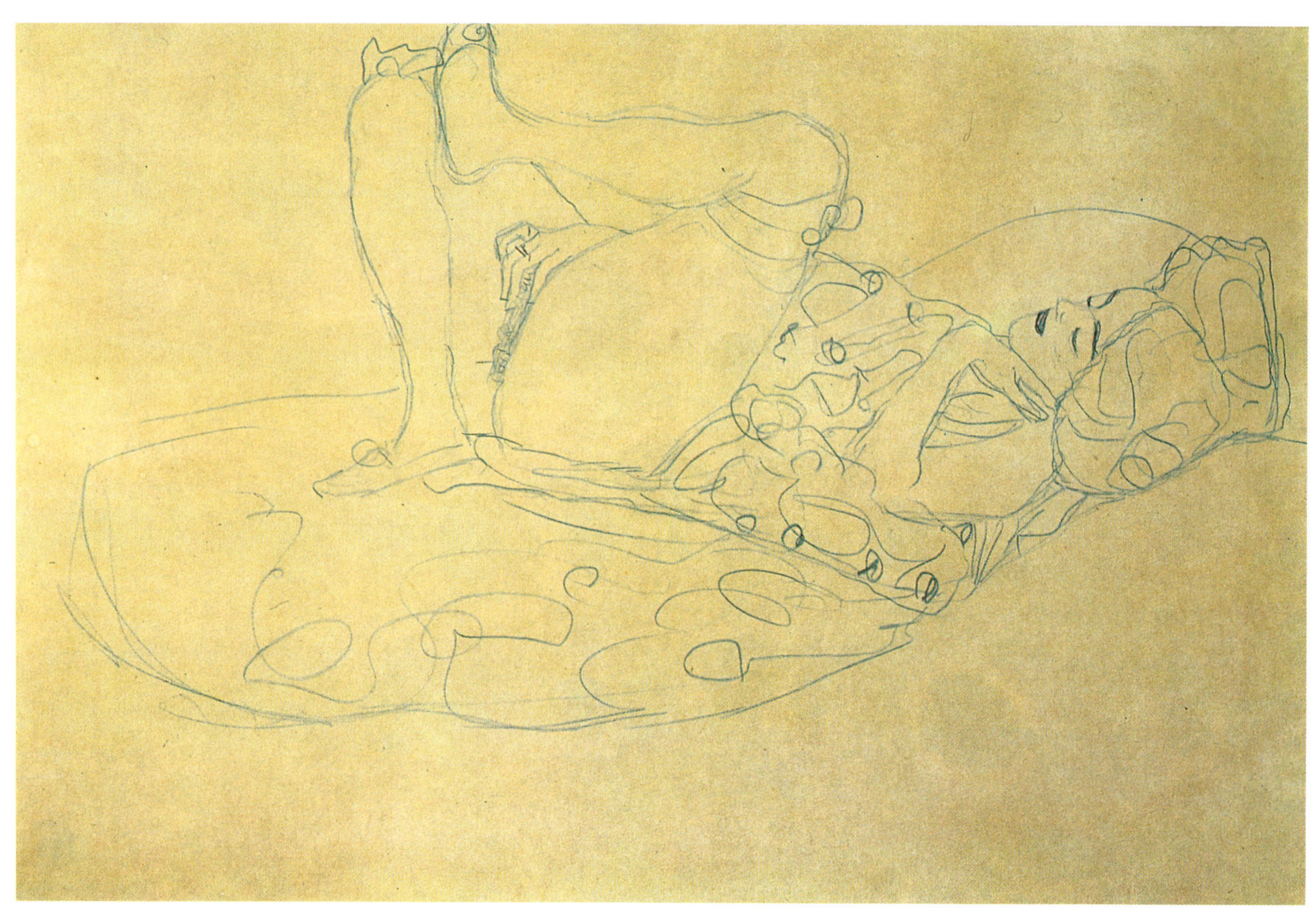

58. ***Semi-nude Lying Down***, 1914. Blue pencil, 37 x 56 cm, Vienna, Historisches Museum.

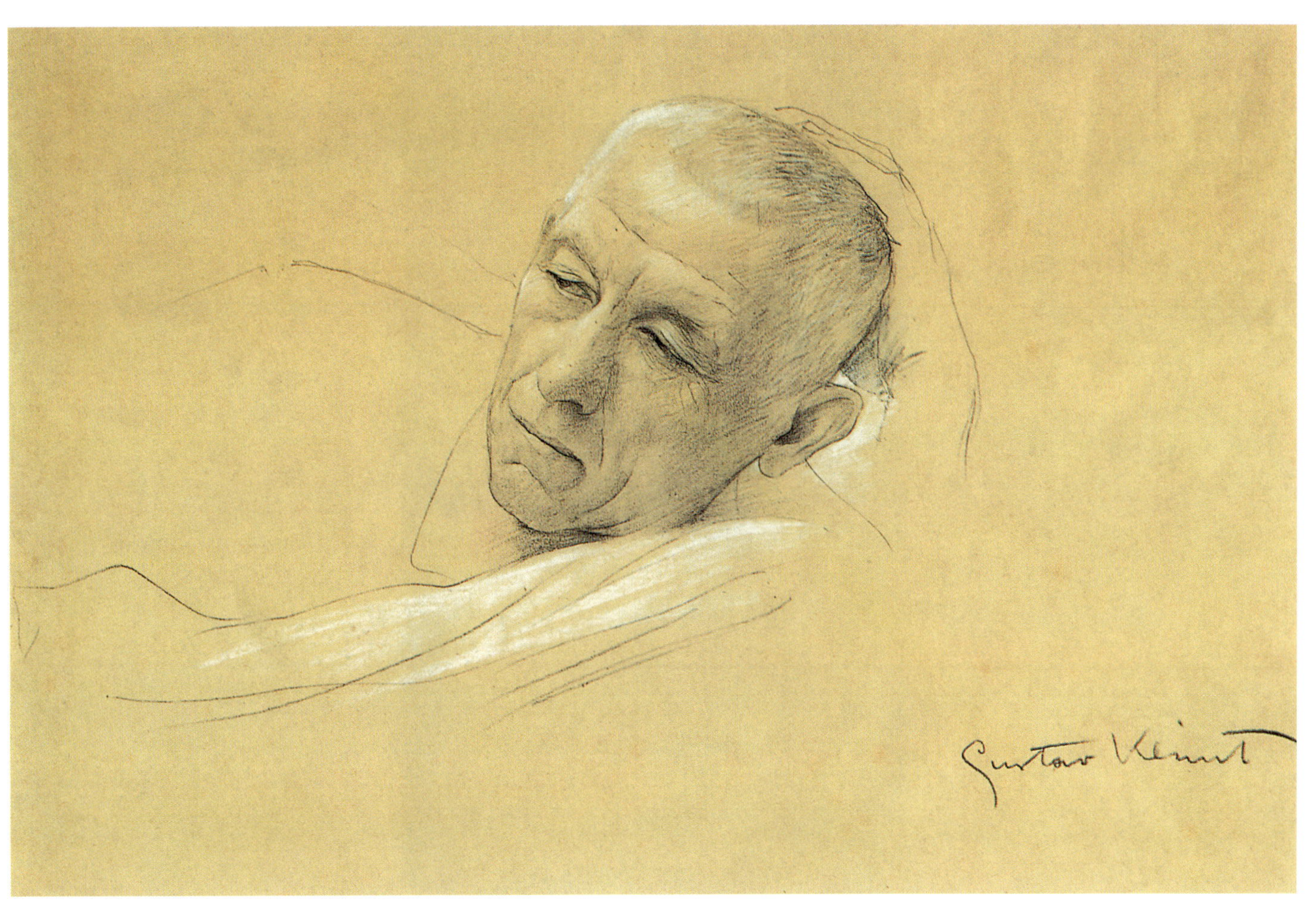

59. ***Man's Head Lying Down*** (painting from the ceiling of the Imperial Venetian Theatre)**,** 1886-1888. Black chalk, white highlights, 28 x 43 cm, Vienna, Albertina.

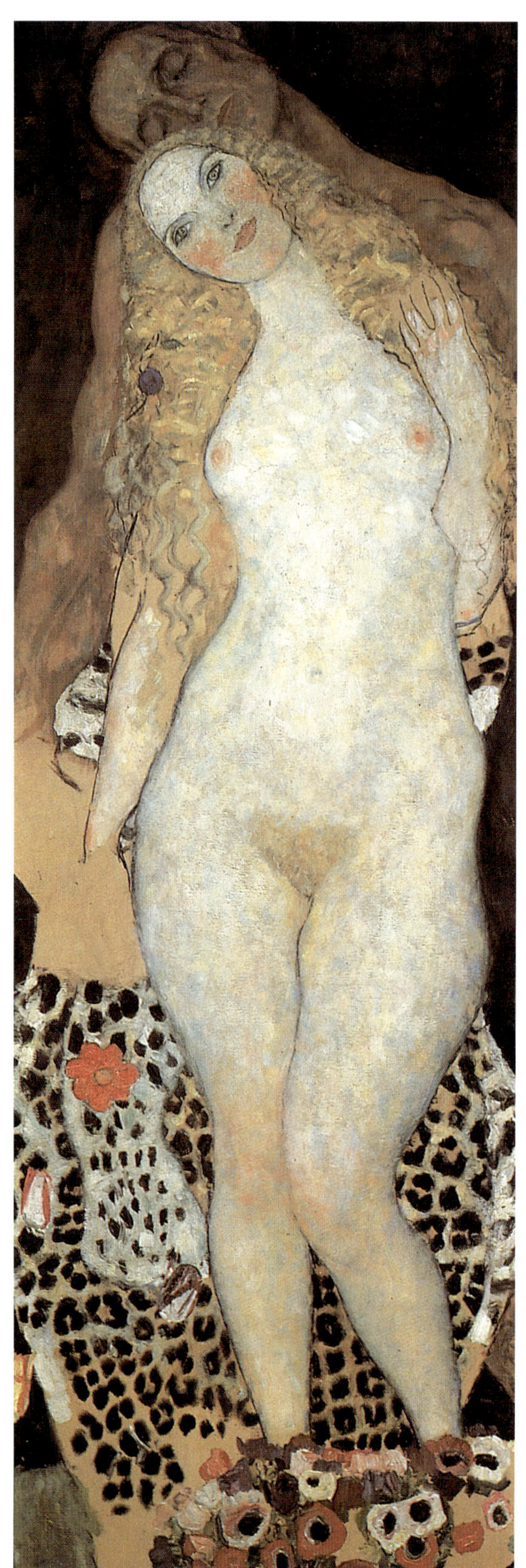

60. ***Adam and Eve (Unfinished)***, 1917-1918. Oil on canvas, 173 x 60 cm, Vienna, Österreichische Galerie.

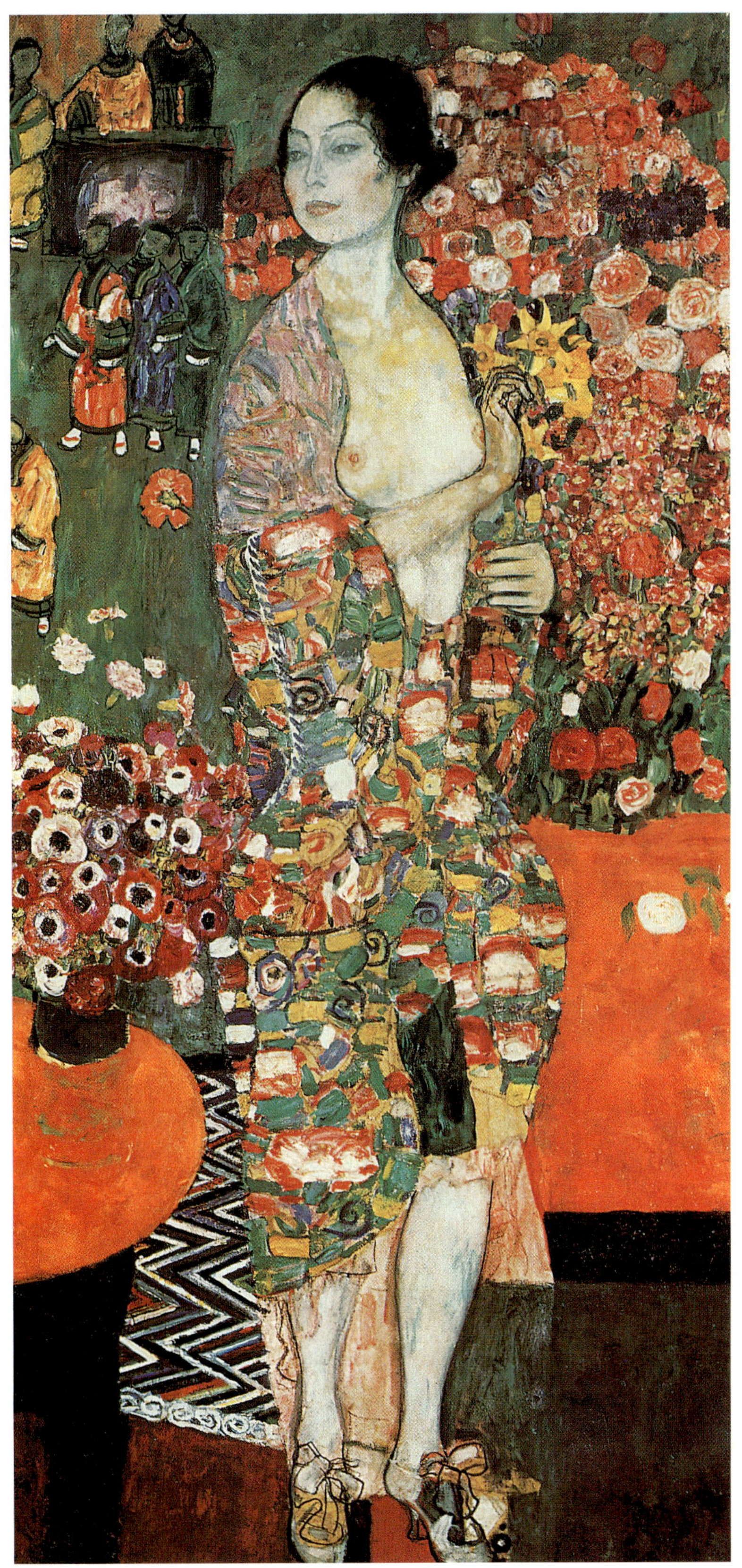

61. ***Dancer***, 1916-1918.
Oil on canvas,
180 x 90 cm,
Private Collection.

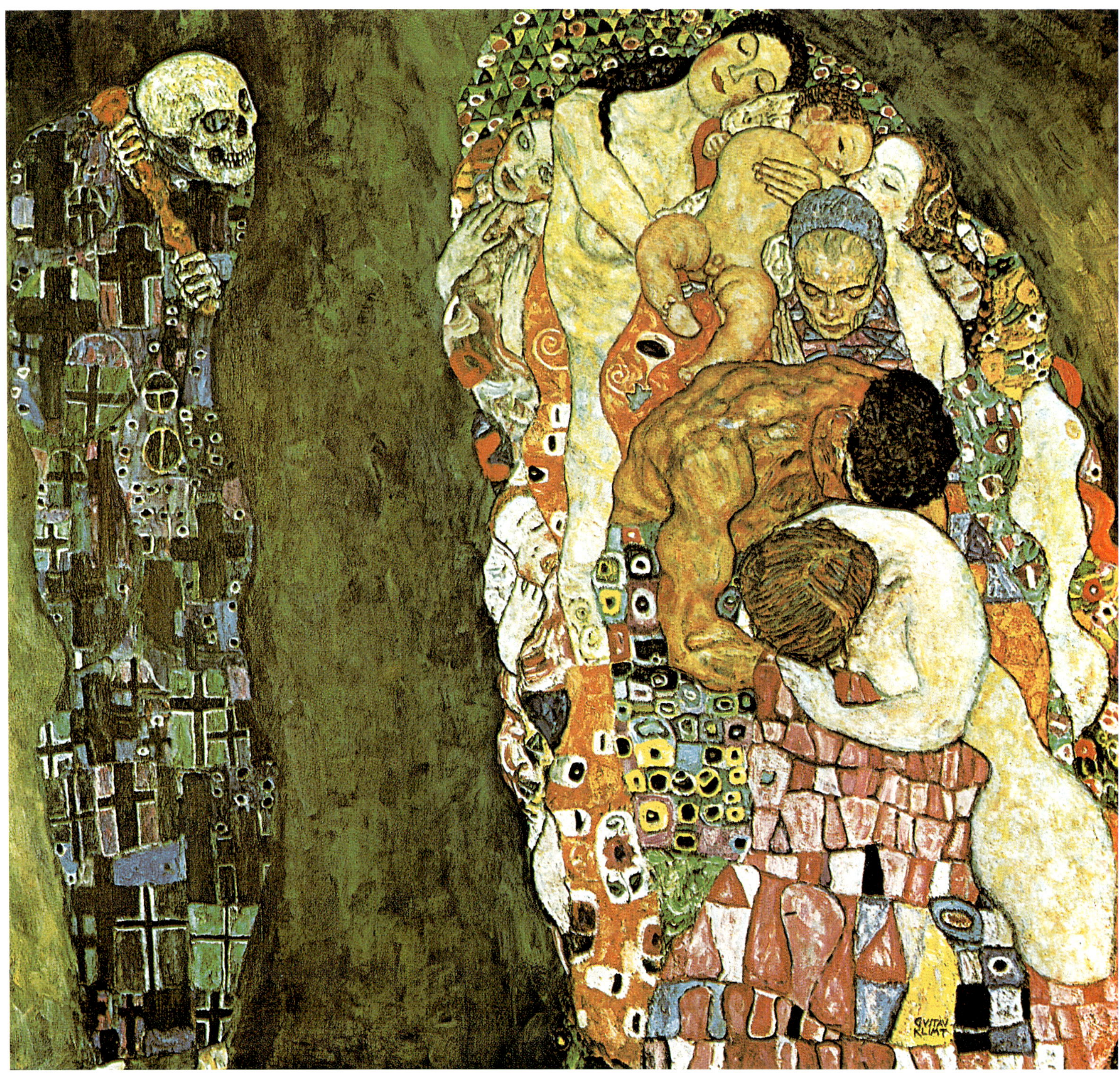

It is as if the women he depicts are imprisoned by the textiles and ornaments, an impression heightened by the artist's heavy use of gold (Klimt had visited Ravenna in 1903, where he had greatly admired the famous Byzantine mosaics).

In *Judith* II (p. 53) the clothes seem barely able to contain the energetic nudity of the avenging woman, and in *Bride* (p. 55) textiles are used as a way of isolating shapes and body parts to create a highly erotic effect.

Heads and torsos become fragmented, detached from their bodies. The figure on the far left of the painting almost resembles Man Ray's photograph of a woman's back as a cello, and the figure to the far right of the canvas has her head totally obscured, leaving her breasts exposed while the lower part of her body is covered by a sexy, see-through skirt leaving her open legs and genitals visible.

The fact that the provocatively naked body exists beneath these skimpy clothes might even suggest, as some of Klimt's preparatory drawings imply, that in other paintings he actually drew the naked body first, then covered it with textiles and pattern.

This, at least, is the impression one has when looking at paintings such as *Virgin* (p. 56) in which the young girl, depicted asleep, is lying prone on her back in a pose at once innocent and sexually exposed.

The clothes look as if they have been thrown on top of her as if to hide her sexual dreams, represented by the mass of semi-naked, presumably more knowing women underneath her.

Klimt's Legacy

During his entire lifetime, Klimt made only one statement about himself and his art: "I am certain that there is nothing exceptional about me as a person.

I am simply a painter who paints every day from morning till night. ... I'm not much good at speaking and writing, especially when I have to discuss myself or my work. Just the idea of having to write a simple letter fills me with anguish.

I am very much afraid that you will have to do without a portrait of me, either painted or in words, but it is no great loss.

62. ***Life and Death***, 1916.
Oil on canvas,
178 x 198 cm, Vienna.

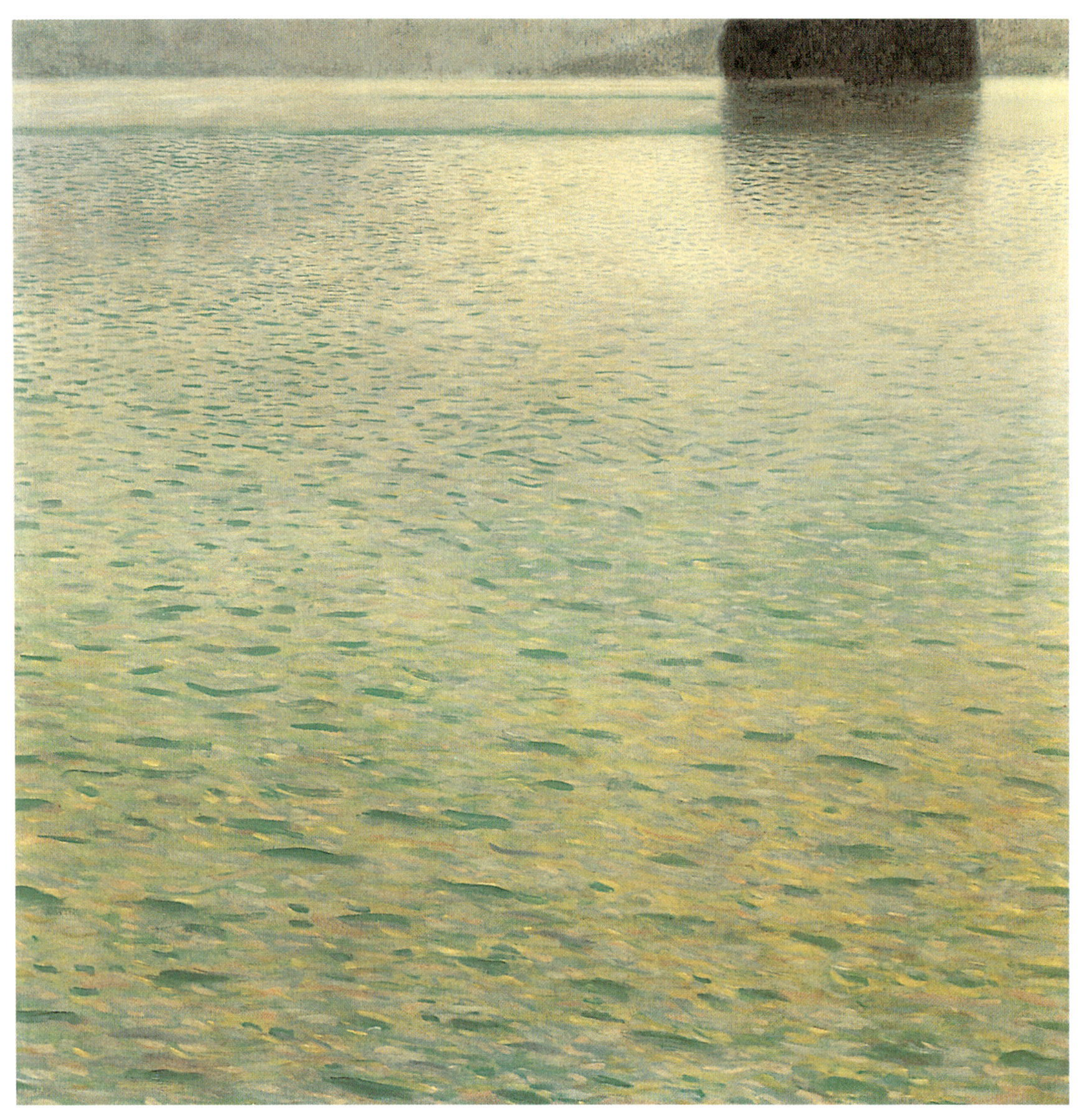

63. ***Island on the Attersee***, about 1901. Oil on canvas, 100 x 100 cm, Private Collection.

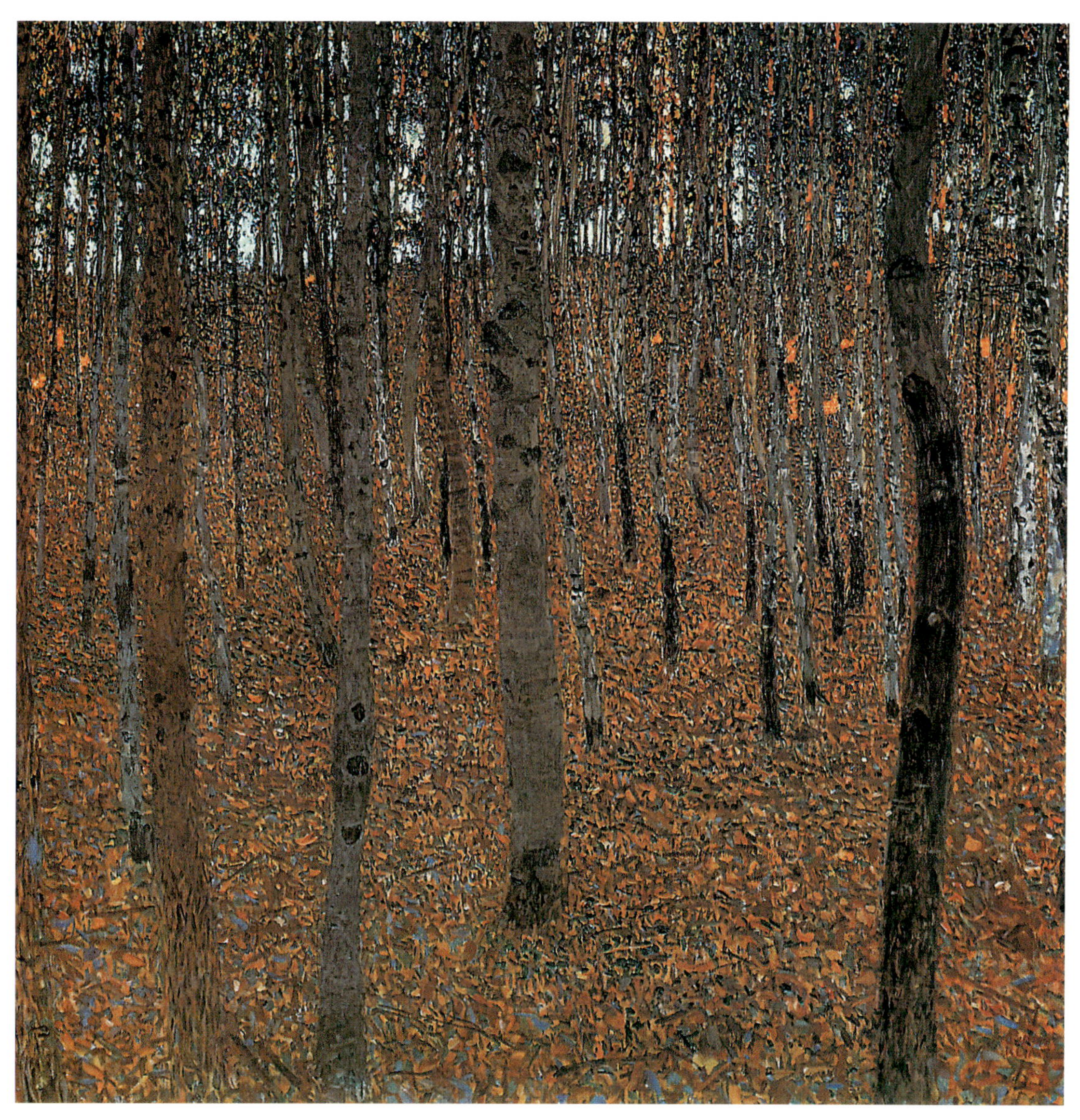

64. ***Forest of Beech Trees I***, about 1902.
Oil on canvas,
100 x 100 cm,
Dresde.

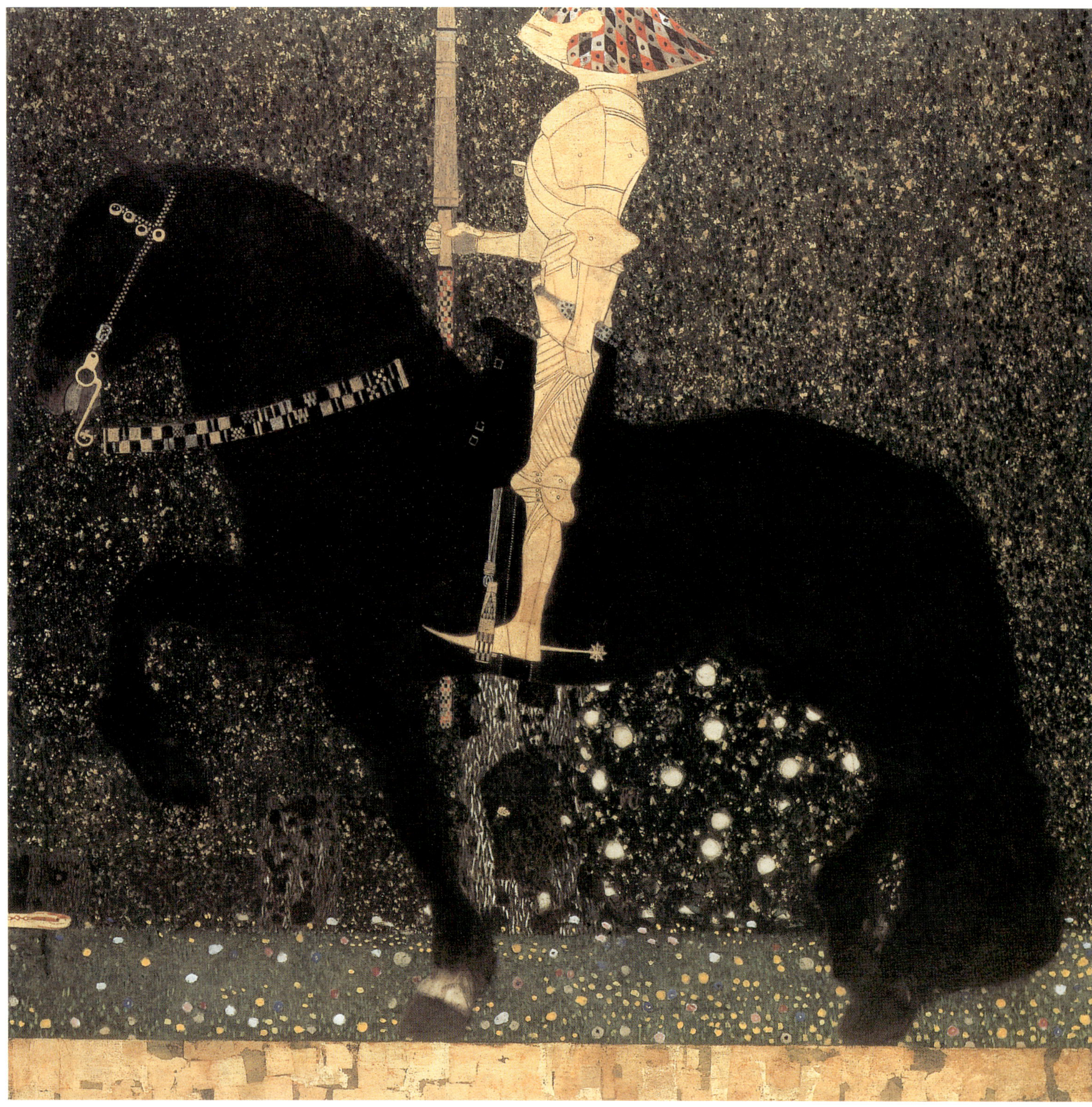

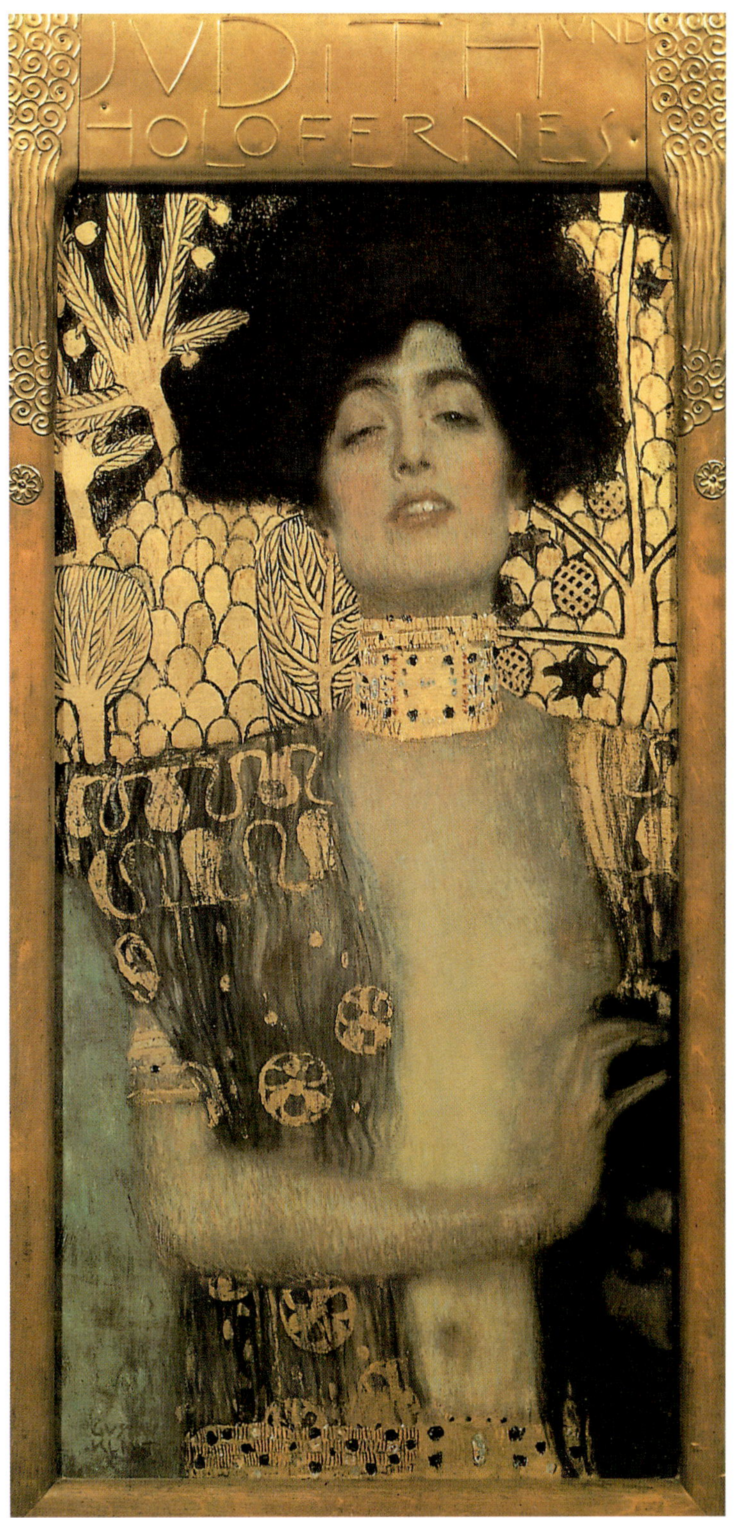

65. ***The Golden Knight***, 1903. Oil, Tempera and gold on canvas, 103.5 x 103.7 cm, Aichi Prefectural Museum of Art, Nagoya, Japan.

66. ***Judith I,*** 1901. Oil on canvas, 84 x 42 cm, Vienna, Östereichische Galerie.

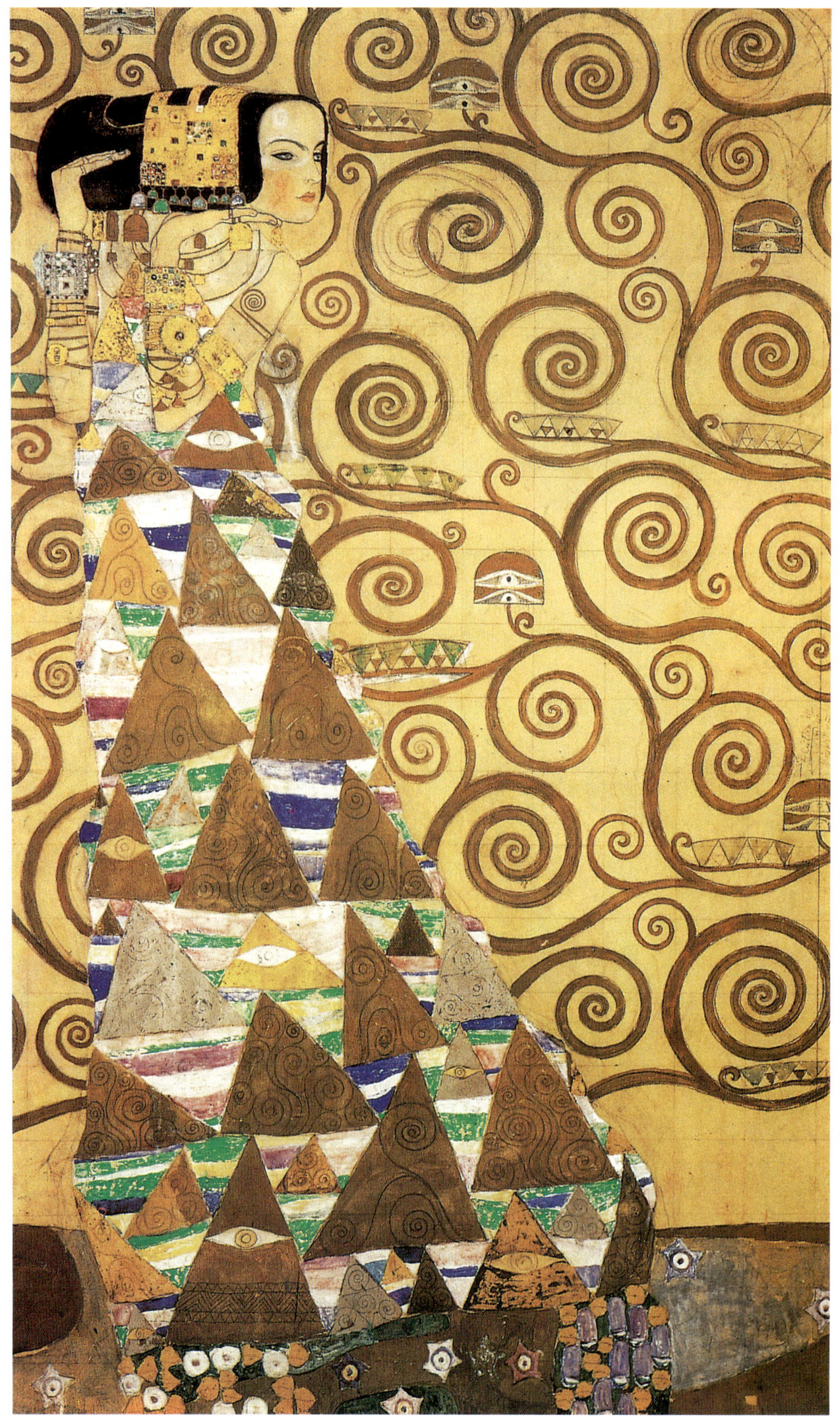

Whoever seeks to know me better, that is to say as an artist - and that's the only thing worth knowing - should study my paintings and try to glean from them who I am and what I want."

Just how exceptional Gustav Klimt was is perhaps reflected in the fact that he had no predecessors and no real followers.

He admired Rodin and Whistler without slavishly copying them, and was admired in turn by the younger Viennese painters Egon Schiele and Oskar Kokoschka, both of whom were greatly influenced by Klimt.

But whereas Klimt belongs to that transitional period at end of the nineteenth century, Schiele and Kokoschka represent the beginnings of that quintessentially early twentieth-century movement, expressionism.

Schiele, like Klimt, made many drawings of nudes, but where Klimt's drawings were peaceful, dreamy and delicate, Schiele reflected a tortured and neurotic psyche.

He drew himself endlessly - an emaciated, troubled figure - and his drawings of female nudes manage to render the women simultaneously sexually attractive and repulsive.

On January 11, 1918, Klimt suffered a stroke that left him partially paralyzed on one side. Although he seemed to be recovering, he died a month later. After his death opinion was still divided as to his merits as an artist.

Hans Tietze, a friend of Klimt and author of the first monograph on the artist, sums up his importance: "Klimt took Viennese painting ... out of the isolation in which it was languishing and back again into the wide world ...

At the turn of the century he, more than anyone else, guaranteed the artistic individuality of Vienna." Klimt, it has been said, could not have existed anywhere but in Vienna. So totally have the images created by him come to represent the Austrian capital at that time that it could indeed be argued that Vienna could not have entered the twentieth century without the bold vision and artistic individuality of Klimt.

67. ***Waiting***, about 1905-1909. Vienna, Österreichisches Museum.

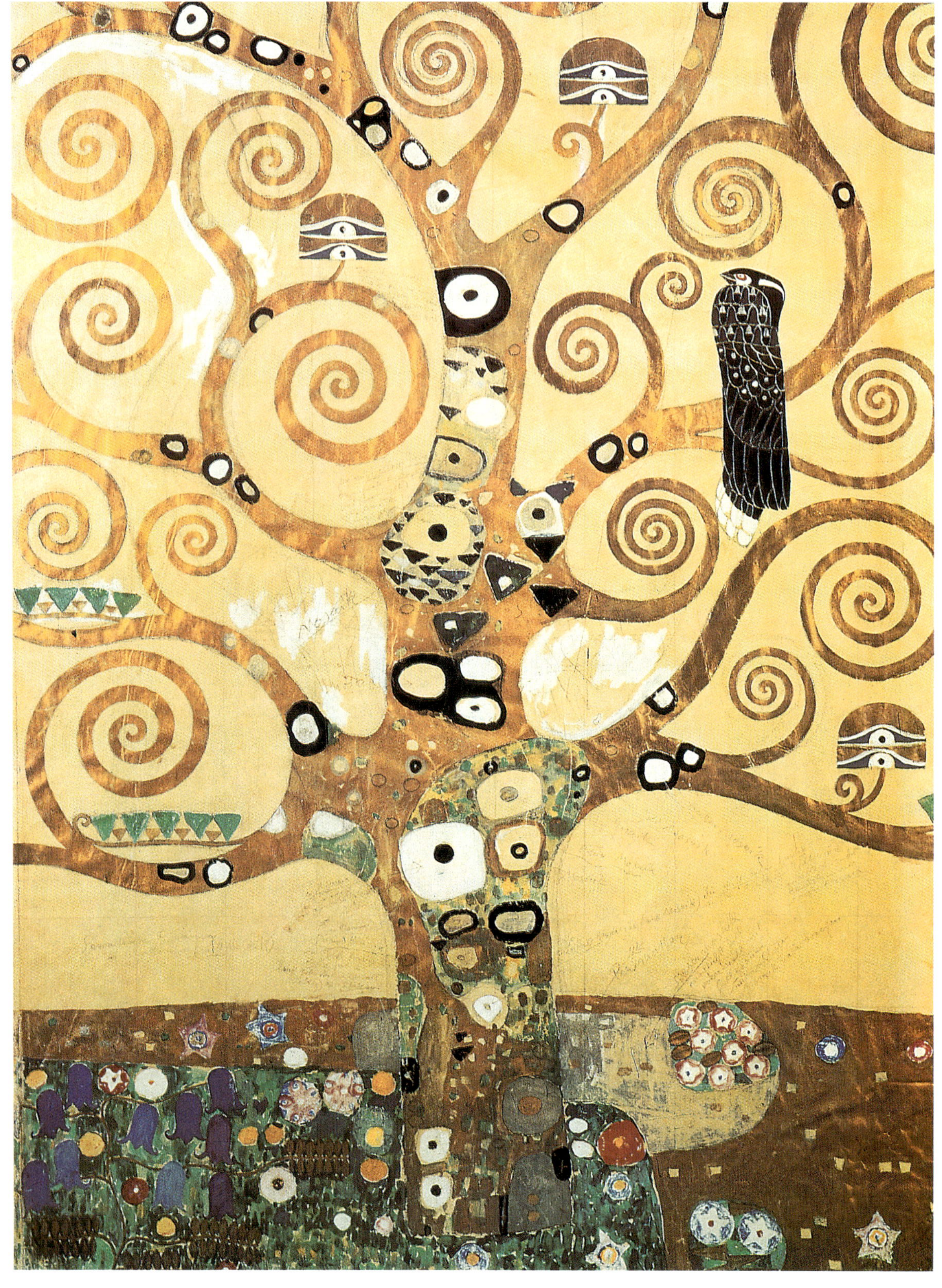

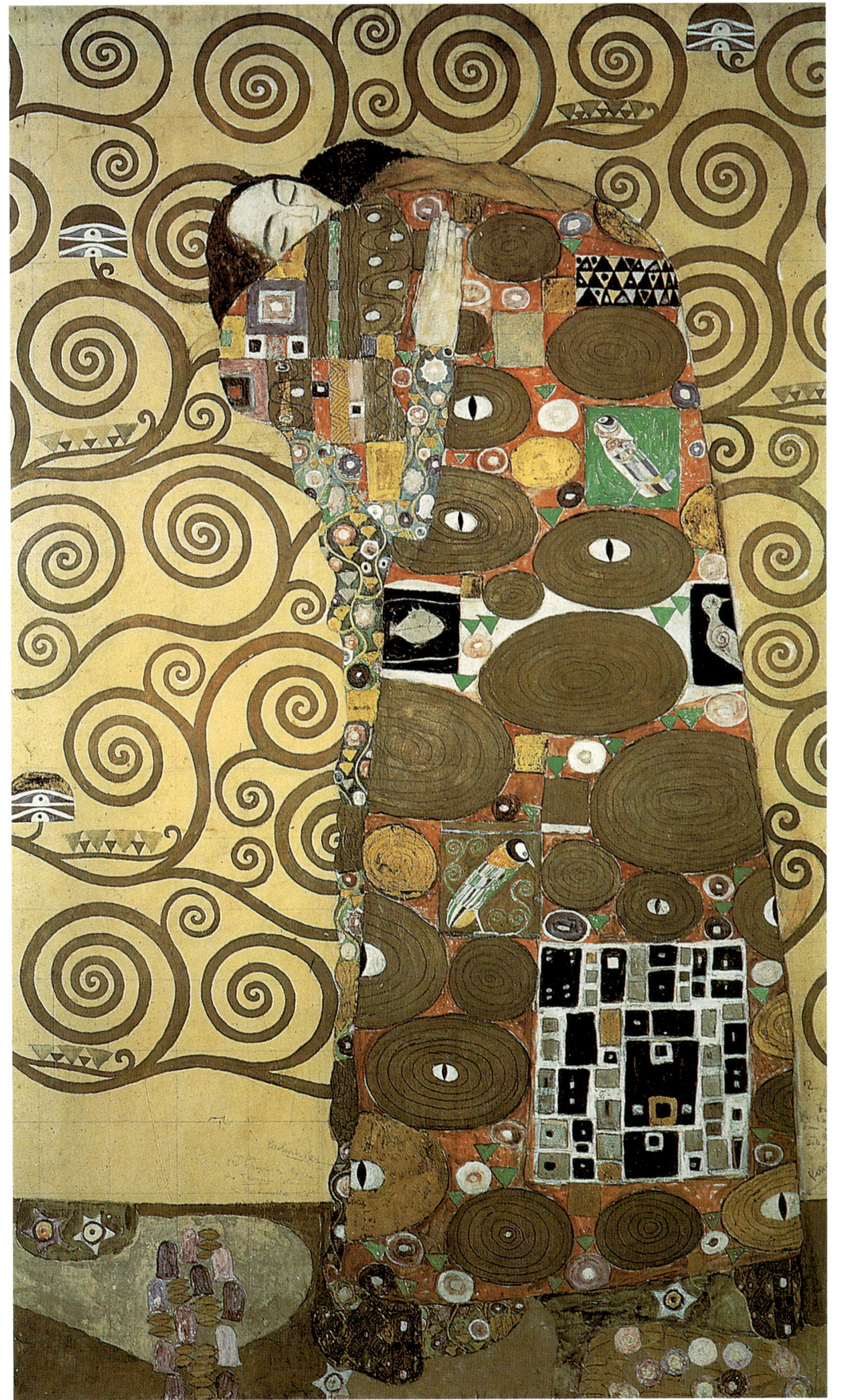

68. ***Tree of Life,*** about 1905-1909. 195 x 102 cm, Vienna, Museum für Angewandte Kunst.

69. ***Accomplishment***, about 1905-1909. Vienna, Österreichisches Museum.

Biography

1862: Birth of Gustav Klimt in Baumgarten, near Vienna. His father, Ernst Klimt was a gold engraver and his mother, Anna Finster, was a lyric singer.

1876: He enters The School of Arts and Sciences at the Museum of Art and Industry in Vienna. He takes painting classes with Professor Laufberger.

1877: To make money, he takes photographic portraits.

1883: Klimt gets his degree from The School of Arts and Sciences in Vienna. He opens a workshop with one of his brothers (Ernst Klimt) and another painter (Franz Matsch). They create several works together, some of which are frescos for theatres.

1885: The group decorates the Hermes villa and the National Theatre of Fiume.

1887: The Municipal Council of Vienna asks Klimt to paint an interior scene in the ancient imperial theatre.

1888: Klimt completes the painting in the imperial theatre. He receives the golden cross of merit.

1889: Klimt begins the decoration of the staircases at the Museum of Art History in Vienna. He receives the Imperial Prize, awarded for the first time to him.

1890: Klimt becomes a member of the group for artists in the plastic arts in Vienna. With his brother Ernst and Franz Matsch, he is awarded "the highest recognition" for the decoration of the Museum of Art History.

1892: His father and his brother Ernst die.

1893: Klimt takes a trip to Hungary where Duke Esterhazy asks him to paint the Totis theatre.

1894: The Minister of Education asks Klimt and Matsch to do the Faculty Paintings on the ceiling of the hallway in the University of Vienna.

1897: Klimt leaves the association for artists in the plastic arts in Vienna. Joseph Maria Olbrich, Josef Hoffmann and Klimt found the Vienna Secession and Klimt becomes the Succession's president. Olbrich, Hoffman and Klimt work on the paintings *Philosophy* and *Medicine* for the University.

70. ***Fish Blood.***

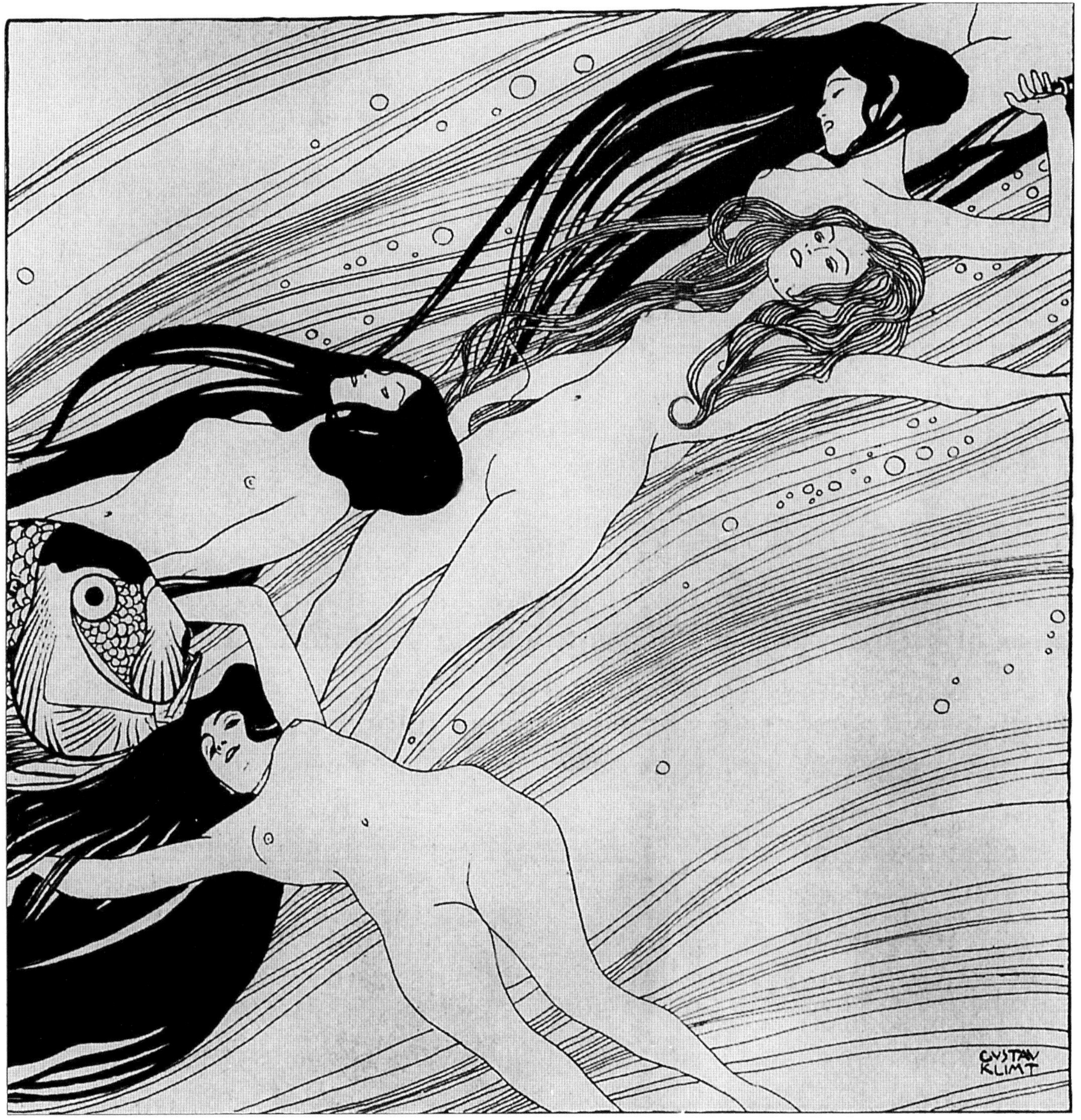
GUSTAV
KLIMT

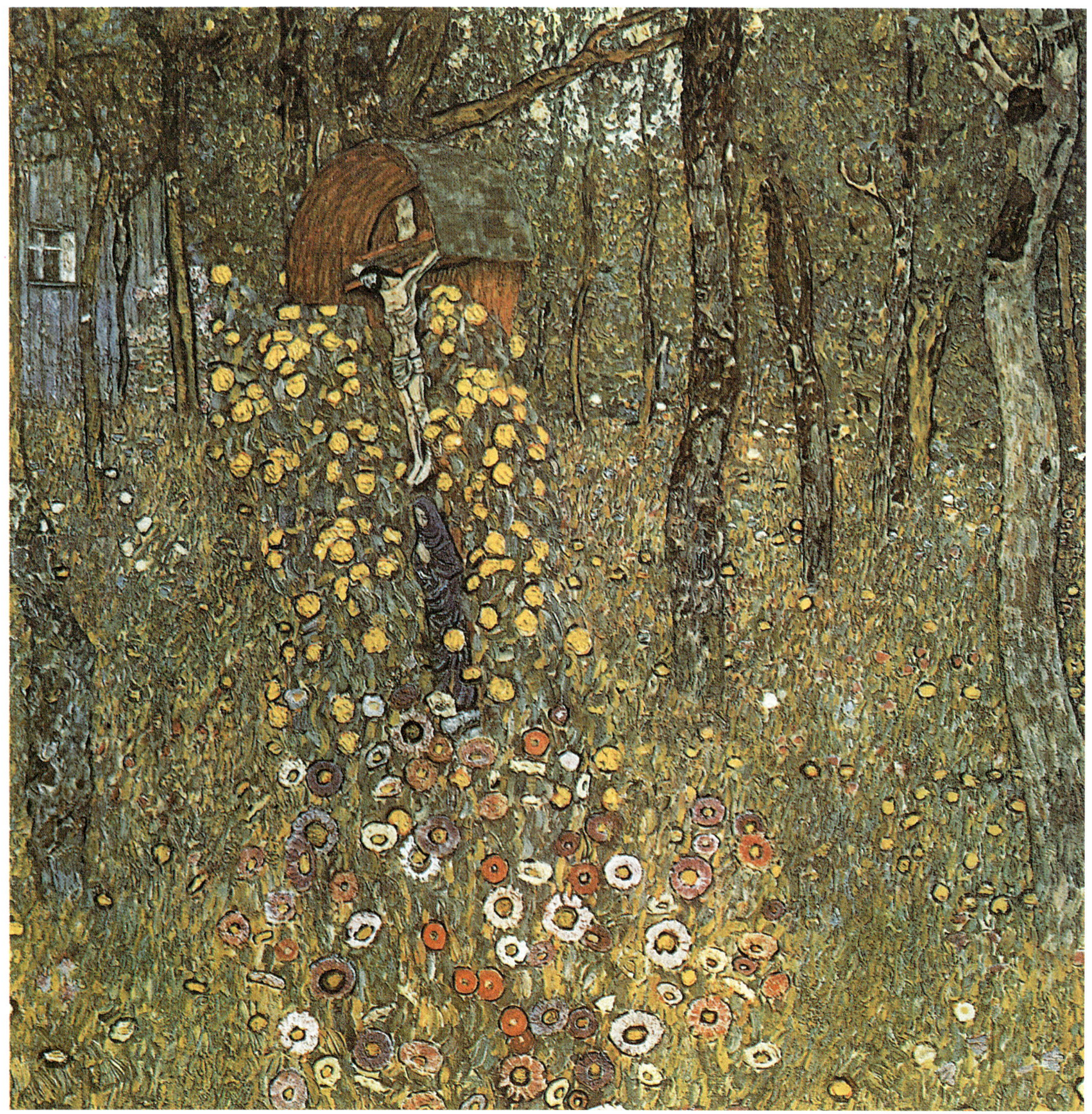

1898: First exposition of the Vienna Secession and the founding of its magazine: *Ver Sacrum*. The same year, Klimt becomes a member of the International Society of Painters, Sculptors and Engravers in London and is nominated a corresponding member of the Munich Succession.

1899: He finishes the decoration for the Music Room at the Dumba palace with his paintings *Schubert at the Piano* and *Music*.

1900: He exhibits, next to landscape paintings, his unfinished *Philosophy* in the Secession's house and the painting provokes violent protests. However, he receives a gold medal for this painting at the World Exhibition in Paris.

1901: The exhibition of *Medicine* receives criticism from the press.

1902: The Secession has an exhibition with a presentation of the Beethoven frieze.

1903: A collective exhibition at the Secession with eighty works by Klimt. Klimt takes a trip to Ravenna and Florence.

1905: The order for the Faculty Paintings is cancelled and then bought back. Klimt retires from the Secession and leaves for Berlin where he participates in the Alliance of German Artists Exhibition with fifteen paintings and receives the "Villa Romana" Prize.

1906: Foundation of the Alliance of Austrian Artists (Klimt becomes president of the Alliance in 1912). He becomes an honorary member of the Royal Bavarian Academy of Decorative Arts in Munich.

1907: He finishes the Faculty Paintings and exhibits them in Vienna and Berlin.

1910: He participates in the Venice Biennial.

1911: Participates, with eight paintings, at the International Exhibition of Art in Rome and receives the first prize for *Life and Death*.

1912: Klimt becomes president of the Alliance of Austrian Artists in Rome.

1917: Klimt becomes an honorary member of the Academy of Decorative Arts in Vienna after a chair had been refused four times by the minister.

1918:
On January 11th, Klimt suffers a stroke in his Viennese apartment and dies on February 6th, leaving a number of unfinished works.

71. ***Garden with crucifix,*** 1911. Oil on canvas, 110 x 110 cm. Burnt in Immendorf castle in 1945.

LIST OF ILLUSTRATIONS